Little River
National Wildlife Refuge

Comprehensive
Conservation
Plan

November 1998

COMPREHENSIVE CONSERVATION PLAN APPROVAL
for the
Little River National Wildlife Refuge
1998

The attached Comprehensive Conservation Plan for the Little River National Wildlife Refuge has been reviewed and approved by the manager of the refuge.

Submitted by:

Berlin Heck   _8/27/98_

Berlin Heck, Refuge Manager
Little River National Wildlife Refuge   Date

Approved by:

Lynn B Starnes   _12/14/98_

Lynn Starnes, Geographic Manager
Texas/Oklahoma   Date

Approved by:

Nancy M. Kaufman   _12/30/98_

Nancy Kaufman   Date
Regional Director, Region 2
U.S. Fish and Wildlife Service

Table of Contents

List of Tables

Section I: Introduction, Planning Approach, and Regional History and Setting

Introduction

This Comprehensive Conservation Plan is prepared for the Little River National Wildlife Refuge in McCurtain County in southeastern Oklahoma. It is an update and revision of a draft Comprehensive Management Plan completed by the U.S. Fish and Wildlife Service in 1991. It has been written to provide continuity of management of Refuge lands for the benefit of wildlife and people.

The Refuge is located in the floodplain of the Little River, extending along approximately 16 miles of the river in an east-west direction (see map, Appendix A). The Little River generally delineates the southern boundary of the Refuge, although several tracts of the Refuge extend to the south of it. There is a gap of approximately 2 miles between the east and west sections of the Refuge where the bottomland timber was removed and the vegetation converted to pine plantations prior to Refuge establishment. Although most of the exterior boundary of the Refuge has been established, there still remain a number of private inholdings that are planned for acquisition as they become available from willing sellers.

The bottomland hardwood ecosystem of the Little River was once a complex and diverse network of plants and animals created and maintained by periodic natural flooding. After years of exploitation and habitat alteration by humans, the lands that comprise the Refuge today differ greatly from the former dynamic and pristine river bottomland ecosystem. Today, Refuge lands consist of a mosaic of regenerated bottomland forest, pine plantations, and young upland hardwood forests. Given time, protection, and proper management, the Refuge bottomlands should regain much of the character of the former riparian forest ecosystem, including a diverse assemblage of plants and animals representative of these declining bottomland hardwood forest habitats.

The Purpose of and Need for Planning

Prior to the early 1800s, over 2 million acres of bottomland hardwood forests existed along the river corridors of eastern Oklahoma. Today only about 15 percent, or 328,700 acres, remains. These remaining bottomland hardwood forests constitute a small fraction of the total land area of the State of Oklahoma, and at the rate of current loss, less than 10 percent of the presettlement total will remain by the year 2015. This loss is due primarily to conversion to pine plantations, development for agriculture,

1

and reservoir construction. Protection, restoration, and maintenance of the bottomland hardwood forest ecosystem on the Little River will contribute significantly to the survival of its biotic communities and to the diversity of the plant and animal communities in southeastern Oklahoma.

The Refuge was established "for use as an inviolate sanctuary, or for any other management purpose, for migratory birds," to conserve wetlands, and "for the development, advancement, management, conservation and protection of fish and wildlife resources."[1] It is intended to contribute towards the preservation of the bottomland hardwood forest ecosystem for the benefit of waterfowl, as well as other migratory birds and wildlife species. Planning is necessary to enhance the Refuge's contributions to overall ecological health within the area of ecological concern and to provide direction for the management and development of the Refuge. The Service's approach is to plan for the achievement of objectives that are consistent with desirable goals for the entire area of ecological concern.[2]

When the Oklahoma House of Representatives and Senate authorized acquisition of the Refuge, they specified ". . . that the United States Fish and Wildlife Service shall enter into a cooperative agreement with the Oklahoma Department of Wildlife Conservation to allow hunting in such waterfowl refuge."[3] Locally, citizens had used the area for fishing and hunting for many years prior to the establishment of the Refuge. The richness of the area's birdlife also makes it a potential site for meeting growing demands for good bird watching sites, with establishment of appropriate access and interpretive facilities.

---

[1] Specific purposes identified in the establishing legislation are found in the following legislative acts: Migratory Bird Conservation Act, 16 U.S.C. 715d: "for use as an inviolate sanctuary, or for any other management purpose, for migratory birds"; Emergency Wetlands Resources Act of 1986, 16 U.S.C. 3901(b), 100 Stat 3583: for "the conservation of the wetlands of the Nation in order to maintain the public benefits they provide and to help fulfill international obligations contained in various migratory bird treaties and conventions..."; and the Fish and Wildlife Act of 1956, 16 U.S.C. 742f(b)(1) and 16 U.S.C. 742f(a)(4): "for the development, advancement, management, conservation, and protection of fish and wildlife resources..for the benefit of the United States Fish and Wildlife Service in performing its activities and Services...."

[2] An area of ecological concern can be defined as: "An essentially complete ecosystem (or set of interrelated ecosystems) of which one part cannot be discussed without considering the remainder" [*Malheur National Wildlife Refuge Master Plan and Environmental Assessment*, 1985, p. 7]. For purposes of the Little River National Wildlife Refuge Comprehensive Conservation Plan, the entire bottomland hardwood forest region of the Mississippi and Arkansas/Red Rivers is considered the area of ecological concern.

[3] House Joint Resolution #1046, signed by Governor George Nigh, March 31, 1986.

Planning
Perspectives

This Comprehensive Conservation Plan identifies goals and objectives for the management of the Refuge, and identifies strategies by which those goals and objectives will be addressed. The plan establishes a practical foundation for preparing budgetary requests, and its implementation will ensure consistency of management over time while providing the flexibility needed to address unanticipated issues as they arise.

This Comprehensive Conservation Plan is designed to enhance and sustain the bottomland hardwood community on the Refuge through an approach to management that considers factors beyond the immediate Refuge boundaries that may affect, or be affected by, the Refuge and its management. This plan:

- Relates the Service's responsibilities for protecting and restoring Refuge bottomland hardwood forest and wetland habitat for both migratory and resident birds, as well as other wildlife species, to regional and area concerns for the overall health of the bottomland hardwood forest ecosystem in southeastern Oklahoma.

- Relates Refuge management to environmental and social concerns, including contaminants, water quality and watershed management, endangered species, biological diversity, community needs, and socioeconomic development.

- Relates activities on the Refuge to policies and legal and regulatory responsibilities of the Service.

- Focuses on what is needed for the Refuge's lands and wildlife to meet Refuge purposes and objectives, and to promote optimal productivity and health of the Refuge bottomland hardwood forest communities.

Objectives of
Comprehensive
Conservation
Planning

The objectives of comprehensive conservation planning are:

- To identify goals and objectives for management of the Refuge, and to specify strategies to achieve those goals and objectives.

- To ensure that management actions address and support the purposes for which the Refuge was established, national policy and the goals of the Refuge System, and the Service's legal and regulatory responsibilities.

- To provide a systematic process for collection, organization, and analysis of data to facilitate management decision-making.

- To provide a framework for monitoring progress and evaluating accomplishments at the Refuge.

- To provide for evaluation of compatibility of existing and potential recreational activities and other public uses on the Refuge, and to ensure National Environmental Policy Act compliance for proposed management actions.

- To ensure that other agencies and the public have opportunities to contribute to management planning for the Refuge.

- To provide a framework for budget requests for operation, maintenance, and capital development programs for the Refuge.

- To provide continuity in the management of the Refuge.

- To ensure that Refuge management considers the ecological context in which the Refuge exists and to help define its future role in maintaining ecosystem health.

Refuge Resource Management Goals

The following is a list of goals that have been identified for the Refuge:

Goal 1: The protection, restoration, and maintenance of the bottomland hardwood forest plant community.

Goal 2: The restoration of native threatened and endangered species through optimum use of Refuge lands.

Goal 3: The protection and enhancement of habitat for migratory bird use.

Goal 4: The protection and enhancement of Refuge habitat to sustain healthy populations of native fish and wildlife species.

Goal 5: Compliance with historic and archeological resource protection laws and regulations.

Goal 6: The development of a biological information database for use in monitoring ecosystem changes and making management decisions.

Goal 7: A public that: (1) enjoys and values fish and wildlife resources found on the Refuge; (2) understands events and issues related to these resources; and (3) acts to promote fish and wildlife conservation.

Goal 8: Expanded recreational hunting and fishing programs.

Goal 9: Efficient administration that supports accomplishment of Refuge objectives.

The Area of Ecological Concern

The bottomland hardwood ecosystem of Oklahoma was once extensive, consisting of an estimated 2.2 million acres. By the early 1980s, approximately 85 percent of those bottomland hardwoods had been destroyed, leaving about 330,000 acres. Southeastern Oklahoma, with its extensive bottomland hardwood habitat along the Red and Little Rivers and their tributaries, was the area most impacted (Brabander et al. 1985)[4].

Since the 1980s, the practice of converting hardwood forests to pine plantations has accelerated the loss. In the early 1990s, the value of hardwoods began to approach that of pines, resulting in removal of much of the remaining bottomland hardwoods for commercial purposes.

By 1995 the three largest expanses of bottomland hardwood habitat remaining in Oklahoma were on federal lands, including this Refuge, the Deep Fork National Wildlife Refuge, and the Tiak Unit of the Ouachita National Forest. There are still remnants of this once dominant ecosystem in private ownership (primarily owned by Weyerhaueser Company), but they are fast disappearing.

The bottomland hardwood ecosystem of eastern Oklahoma is dynamic. Periodic flooding keeps the lower elevations of the floodplain continually in flux. The Little River meanders through the floodplain, changing its

---

[4] Brabander, J.J., Masters, R.E., and Short, R.M. 1985. Bottomland hardwoods of eastern Oklahoma: A special study of their status, trends and values. U.S. Fish and Wildlife Service.

course as the force of flood water first cuts into banks, then creates cutoffs that form oxbow lakes. Flooding, erosion, and deposition of silt raise and lower land elevations and leave behind seasonal and "permanent" ponds, and saturated soils that accommodate only those plants most tolerant of high soil moisture. On better drained soils, a different but equally varied plant community thrives.

This periodic inundation results in a bottomland hardwood community in various stages of succession. Historically, this association ranged from the permanently flooded cypress community to the periodically flooded oak-hickory woodland. Flooding of river bottomlands has been essential to the maintenance of the plant species native to bottomland forests.

The north side of the Little River is characterized by freshwater marshes, sloughs, small shallow flooded woodlands, spring-fed creeks, and old river oxbows. Most of the Refuge lies on the low-lying north side of the Little River. South of the river, limestone bluffs rise 50 to 100 feet above the flat, sedimentary bottomland.

History of Little River
National Wildlife Refuge

The Refuge was established on February 10, 1987, primarily to preserve wetlands, as a sanctuary for migratory birds, "for the development, advancement, management, conservation and protection of fish and wildlife resources." The Refuge serves to preserve one of the last remaining remnants of the once extensive bottomland hardwood ecosystem of the Little River floodplain. When land purchases and exchanges are completed, the Refuge will contain 15,000 acres that have a potential for full restoration to a mature and biologically diverse bottomland hardwood forest ecosystem.

Climate

Stanley Holbrook, climatologist for the Oklahoma National Weather Service, describes the climate as follows:[5] "McCurtain County has a warm, moist subtropical climate. Air masses from the Gulf of Mexico play the dominant role in influencing the weather, although cool, moist air masses from the Pacific and cold, dry air masses from Canada and the Arctic Circle frequent the area during the winter months. Seasonal changes are gradual. The spring and autumn months are mild, with cool nights and

---

[5] Soil Survey, McCurtain County, Oklahoma, USDA, Soil Conservation Service, in cooperation with Oklahoma Agricultural Experiment Station. November 1974, page 95.

warm days. Summers are hot. Winters are mild, but well defined. Long periods of severe cold are infrequent.

"Precipitation averages 47 inches per year at Idabel . . . and it is well distributed throughout the year. Spring is the wettest season, receiving 31 percent of the average yearly precipitation. Autumn is the driest season, with 21 percent . . . . Snowfall is generally light. On an average 2 to 4 inches of snow falls each year and seldom remains on the ground more than two days . . . . Prevailing winds are southerly, with an average speed of 12 miles per hour. Strong winds associated with thunderstorms are most common during the spring season."

Hydrology

The Little River drains a watershed of approximately 2,225 square miles. It originates in southwest LeFlore County, Oklahoma, and flows first westerly and then south and east through Pushmataha and McCurtain Counties into Arkansas where it joins the Red River. The Little River has two major tributaries in Oklahoma: The Glover River joins the Little River approximately 12 miles west of the Refuge boundary, and the Mountain Fork River joins the Little River in the eastern part of the Refuge. A number of smaller creeks also flow into the river, including Holly Creek, Lukfata Creek, Yashau Creek, Yanubbee Creek, Terrapin Creek, and Crooked Creek.

Most of the Refuge is located within the 100-year floodplain, and much of the area still floods every few years. Refuge ground elevations generally range from 330 to 350 feet above sea level, but reach as high as 400 feet above sea level on the south side of the river.

The 100-year flood elevation, as determined by the U.S. Army Corps of Engineers, is 352.7' National Geodetic Vertical Datum at the Highway 259 Bridge.

Construction of dams has considerably altered the flooding regimes of the Little River and its tributaries. Pine Creek Dam, which impounds the Little River approximately 30 river miles upstream of the Refuge, has moderated downstream flooding. To the north of the Refuge, the Mountain Fork River has been impounded by Broken Bow Reservoir, the only major impoundment on the Mountain Fork River. Below the Refuge, DeQueen, Dierks, Gillham, and Millwood dams have reduced the flooding frequency of the Little River. These dams have changed the overall hydrology of the Little River, and may eventually trigger changes in composition of the bottomland hardwood association.

Other changes in the watershed have affected flooding patterns. Some forestry management practices, road construction, agricultural practices, urbanization, and other land developments have resulted in more erosion and more turbid water conditions. Several elevated bridge approaches across the Little River floodplain also serve as barriers to the movement of flood water. Frequency and duration of inundation in the floodplain is believed to have greatly changed.

Vegetation

The bottomland hardwood forest ecosystem of southeastern Oklahoma is characterized by a diversity of plants. Woodlands in areas with regularly saturated soil contain a variety of water-tolerant species. A complex mixture of maples, oaks, and other hardwood species of all ages occupy somewhat higher ground.

The vegetative communities present today have been altered from the hardwood forest ecosystem that once existed in the Little River floodplain. Today the river bottomlands are a mosaic of open river, streams, oxbows, beaver ponds, cutover areas regenerating with dense brush or replanted to pines, and bottomland hardwood forest. Plant associations occurring on the Refuge include those found in:

- Seasonally flooded areas of permanently saturated soils where cypress trees predominate and sparse emergent vegetation forms the understory, particularly planer elm, buttonbush, and black willow.

- Seasonally flooded bottomlands, where soils are not permanently saturated, which support primarily willow oak, cherrybark red oak, overcup oak, shumard oak, water oak, and white oak in the overstory. Understory species include mulberry, redbud, dogwood, huckleberry, holly, hornbeam, maple, poison ivy, greenbriars, grapes, and honeysuckle.

- Mature riparian forest of oaks (water, willow, white, southern red) sugar maples, hackberry, sweet gum, nutmeg hickories, and other trees that are more than 70 years old.

- Bottomlands that were cleared of native oak forests and converted to pine plantations for accelerated growth and harvest.

- Uplands above the floodplain, consisting of mature oak/hickory forest.

Wildlife

The Little River bottomland hardwood ecosystem supports a diversity of wildlife including both resident and migratory species (see Appendix B). It is an important migration stop for many species of neotropical birds and provides suitable nesting habitat for others. Herons and egrets nest in several rookeries on the Refuge. The only known nesting site remaining in the state for the Swainson's warbler is on the Refuge, where a sizeable population occurs. The Refuge has also recorded the only regular nesting location in the state for anhingas.

The Refuge represents the farthest northern expansion of the American alligator in Oklahoma. Two species of amphibians, the bird-voiced treefrog and the mole salamander, are found only on the Refuge as disjunct or isolated populations, separated from their normal range by more than 150 miles.

Waterfowl using the Refuge in large numbers include mallards, wood ducks, gadwall, wigeon, and green-winged teal. Many other species may be found in smaller numbers. The wood duck regularly uses cavities in mature cypress trees on the Refuge as nest sites.

Soils

Flooding patterns have largely determined the nature of soils in the bottomland hardwood forest ecosystems. The most common soil type is the deep, nearly level, poorly drained silt-loam soils of the Guyton series found in the floodplains and terraces of the Little River. This soil has very low permeability (less than 1 inch per hour), with the seasonal water table varying from the surface to 1 foot below the surface. Thus, the available water capacity is high. The shrink-swell potential of this soil is low to moderate. Corrosability on steel pipe is high (pH is 5.1 to 6.0). The soil depth is greater than 72 inches and its profile is as follows:

0 inches to 4 inches	-	Dark grayish brown silt loam
4 inches to 16 inches	-	Light brownish gray silt loam
16 inches to 38 inches	-	Gray silty clay loam

Soils subject to flooding and formed in loamy sediment are either deep brown loam underlain by clay loam, or fine, sandy loam (Rexor and Ochlockonee series). These have moderate to moderately rapid permeability with high available water capacity. Upland areas not subject to flooding are primarily characterized by fine sandy loam and sandy clay loam (Cahaba and Ruston series).

Air Quality

Air quality in southeastern Oklahoma is very high, as can be expected in a sparsely settled county that has little industry. The Refuge is designated as Class 1 land under the guidelines provided in the 1977 Clean Air Act, a classification that contains provisions to maintain high air quality. All

Refuge activities and facilities that may impact air quality must be conducted in accordance with the Act, comply with state air quality standards, and, where appropriate, be monitored according to state requirements.

Mineral, Oil, and Gas Resources

All mineral rights on Refuge lands were retained by prior owners. At the present time, there are no mineral, oil, or gas developments on the Refuge and no identified deposits.

Human History and Cultural Resources

Prehistoric: The Little River area was on the fringe of two major cultural areas, the Plains and the Eastern Woodlands. Elements of both cultural traditions are reflected in the archeological record. The Little River area was within the range of Caddoan-speaking groups, who are believed to have originated in the southeastern woodlands and gradually moved out into the plains late in the prehistoric period.

In recent years the Oklahoma Archeological Survey has recorded 19 cultural sites on the Refuge and has documented 18 unrecorded "leads" on the Refuge. These sites include prehistoric Caddaon mound sites and villages as well as historic Choctaw homesteads. Nearly all of these sites have been damaged or destroyed as a result of modern forestry practices prior to Refuge establishment. Few, if any, of the known sites are undisturbed.

Archeological investigations in the Little River region date from the 1930s and have yielded considerable information on the Archaic, Woodland, and Prehistoric Villager (Caddoan) periods. There is little evidence currently available for the Paleo-Indian era, as is the case for the aboriginal historic period.

A number of Archaic Period sites, some with stratified deposits, have been identified regionally on the basis of tool assemblages and a limited series of chronometric dates. The data point to a substantial occupation of the region by hunter-gatherer groups between 6000 B.C. and 1000 B.C.

Stratigraphic findings at several late Archaic sites in southeastern Oklahoma suggest that these same hunting-gathering populations gradually became the region's prehistoric farmers. Traits indicative of an increasingly sedentary, horticultural lifestyle begin to appear in the archeological record by about A.D. 100. Pottery, groundstone items, and arrow points dominate the material trait profile by A.D. 600, and the ensuing era of early sedentary horticulturist is labeled the Woodland (Fourche Maline) or "Pre-Caddoan Period."

Beginning about A.D. 800, the region is believed to have been occupied in agricultural hamlets and villages by people ancestral to the historic Caddo. The earlier Woodland farmers acquired material traits (e.g., engraved pottery designs, increased mortuary ceremonialism) indicative of the emerging Mississippian Tradition, which in southeastern Oklahoma is referred to specifically as the Caddo Period. The most substantial Caddoan occupation was in the lower Little River drainage and the Red River, where farmsteads and small hamlets were the norm. The Caddo era, which lasted to the time of European contact, is marked by mound building and status burial practices throughout most of the prehistoric period.

Late in the prehistoric sequence, and on into the historic era, most of southeast Oklahoma lay uninhabited by native populations. During the exploration of the Little River by LaHarpe in 1719-1720, no Caddoan villages were reported as inhabited or visited. The region was apparently an uninhabited zone between the Osage to the north, the Wichita to the west, and Caddo in the Red River Valley. The Ouachita mountains and the Little River area may have been visited by Apache and Choctaw hunting parties, in addition to wide-ranging Caddo hunters who were using the area as their hunting grounds.

Historic: In 1820, much of southeastern Oklahoma was conveyed to the Choctaw and Creek Indians of Alabama and Mississippi, in exchange for lands they owned in Alabama and Mississippi by treaty with the United States.

McCurtain County was formed out of the Choctaw Nation in 1825 and was named for a well-known Choctaw Indian family of which the father and his three sons all served as chief of the Choctaw Nation. The county has the oldest farm, oldest church, and oldest post office in Oklahoma.

Beginning in the early 1800s, settlers began to use the forest resources. Mature trees were cut to make wheels, barrels, wagons, furniture, and other items. Much of the land was cleared for agriculture with corn and cotton being raised in most areas. As the population slowly increased, the timber industry, farming, and livestock production became the primary means of support for citizens.

During the mid-1900s, major timber companies such as Dierks and Weyerhaeuser moved in to begin modern forestry practices, taking advantage of the hundreds of thousands of acres of timber in the county. Also, a major chicken industry became established, with growers scattered throughout the region.

A tourism industry began to flourish in the county, and tourism is now one of the major economic industries in the county.

Socioeconomic Setting

McCurtain County encompasses 1,167,846 acres. The population of McCurtain County is approximately 33,500, of which nearly one-third reside in Idabel and Broken Bow. Approximately 65 percent of the population is white, 21 percent American Indians and 14 percent African Americans. Over 29 percent of the population are children, many of them from single parent families. Due to a high unemployment rate, McCurtain County is classified by the State of Oklahoma as a Labor Surplus Area.

Most of McCurtain County's acreage is commercial woodlands managed by large forest products companies. For years, forest products had been important to the county's economy. Since Weyerhaeuser Company began operations in the county in the 1970s, more than half a million acres of hardwoods have been converted to pine plantations, creating a major forest products industry that includes several sawmills, a paper mill, a particle board plant and a plywood plant.

Other leading industries in the county include grain farming, and beef and poultry production. Major crops, in order of importance, are wheat, sorghum, soybeans, and corn. The county ranks first in Oklahoma in beef cattle production and fourth in cow/calf production. The county has led the state in the poultry industry since Tyson Foods, Inc., began operating a poultry processing plant in the area in 1986.

Two Corps of Engineers reservoirs in the area, Broken Bow and Pine Creek, provide water-related recreation. Their clear water and attractive scenery draw tourists from a wide area to McCurtain County. Within a 25-mile radius of the Refuge, ample opportunity exists for hunting, fishing, camping, boating, swimming, and picnicking. Thousands of acres are available for recreation on the Ouachita National Forest, and much of the land owned by forest products companies is presently available for public recreation. The Forest Heritage Center Museum and Beavers Bend Nature Center, both at Beavers Bend State Park, about 12 miles north of the Refuge, are the only natural history interpretive facilities in the area. The Museum of the Red River, in Idabel, exhibits Indian artifacts.

Section II: Legal and Regulatory
Mandates and Guidelines

Legal Mandates

Administration of national wildlife refuges is governed by various federal statutes, as well as by regulations and Presidential executive orders. A list of the most pertinent statutes establishing legal parameters and policy direction for the National Wildlife Refuge System is included in Appendix C, along with a summary of those laws that provide special guidance and have strong implications for the Service and for national wildlife refuges. For the bulk of laws and other mandates, legal summaries are available upon request.

Agency-Wide
Policy Directions

The Fish and Wildlife
Service Mission

While the Service mission and purpose have been evolving since the early 1900s, it has always been tied to a national commitment to wildlife. President Roosevelt established the first national wildlife refuge in 1903 by Executive order. Pelican Island became a refuge for herons and egrets--then under threat of extinction due to the demands for their plumes for the millinery trade. Establishment of several other refuges to preserve nesting islands and rookeries or special habitat followed in rapid succession. In 1905, 2 years before Oklahoma became a state, Wichita Mountains Wildlife Refuge joined Yellowstone National Park (established in 1872) as a second preserve for the American bison, whose numbers had diminished during the 19th century from millions to a few hundred. Thus began the commitment of public lands for the preservation of migratory birds and other wildlife.

The Service's responsibilities broadened during the 1930s. As a result of drought, drainage of wetlands for agriculture, and unregulated hunting, waterfowl populations nationwide became severely depleted. Passage of the Migratory Bird Hunting and Conservation Stamp Act in 1934 made funds available to purchase acreage for waterfowl habitat. During the next several decades, the special emphasis of the Service (then called the Bureau of Sport Fisheries and Wildlife) became the restoration of migratory waterfowl populations.

The passage of the Endangered Species Act in 1973 refocused the activities of the Service and other government agencies. This Act mandated the protection and conservation of threatened and endangered species of fish, wildlife, and plants, both through federal action and by encouraging the establishment of state programs. A myriad of other conservation-related laws soon followed, including the Fish and Wildlife Conservation Act of 1980, which emphasized the conservation of nongame species and broadened management responsibilities for all the national wildlife refuges. In 1974, the Bureau of Sport Fisheries and Wildlife was renamed the U.S. Fish and Wildlife Service and was assigned new responsibilities for endangered and nongame species. Lands continued to be added to the Refuge System for various wildlife protection purposes including endangered species.

The Fish and Wildlife Service's mission is derived from a multitude of laws (see Appendix C), and treaties with Canada and Mexico that collectively outline the role of the federal government with respect to wildlife conservation. The Department of the Interior Departmental Manual states:

> "The U.S. Fish and Wildlife Service is responsible for conserving, enhancing, and protecting fish and wildlife and their habitats for the continuing benefit of people through Federal programs relating to wild birds, endangered species, certain marine mammals, inland sport fisheries, and specific fishery and wildlife research activities."[6]

Mission of the National Wildlife Refuge System

The National Wildlife Refuge System Improvement act of 1997 defines the mission of the national wildlife refuges as: "To administer a national network of lands and waters for the conservation, management, and where appropriate, restoration of the fish, wildlife, and plant resources and their habitats within the United States for the benefit of present and future generations of Americans."[7]

Refuge Purpose Statements

The legislation or executive order that establishes each refuge defines the purposes for its creation. Purpose statements are used as the basis for

---

[6] Departmental Manual, 2 AM 2, Organization, 142 DM 1.1.

[7] National Wildlife Refuge System Improvement Act of 1997 (Public Law 105-57, October 9, 1997).

determining primary management activities, and for determining allowable uses of refuges through a formal "compatibility" process.[8]

Little River National Wildlife Refuge was established as "...an inviolate sanctuary, or any other management purpose, for migratory birds"[9] for "the conservation of...wetlands...and to help fulfill international obligations contained in various migratory bird treaties and conventions,"[10] and "for the development, advancement, management, conservation, and protection of fish and wildlife resources...."[11] Oklahoma House Joint Resolution #1046, which approved the establishment of the Refuge by the U.S. Fish and Wildlife Service, further indicated that the purpose of the Refuge was for "preservation of bottomland hardwood habitat for migratory waterfowl, particularly mallards and wood ducks."[12]

---

[8] A use may be determined to be compatible if it will not have a detrimental effect upon fulfillment of the purposes of the refuge unit and the National Wildlife Refuge System.

[9] 16 U.S.C. 715d.

[10] 16 U.S.C. 3901(b).

[11] 16 U.S.C. 742(b)(1).

[12] House Joint Resolution #1046, signed by Oklahoma's Governor George Nigh, March 31, 1986.

A mature, riparian forest of oaks, maples, hickories and other hardwood species is found on higher ground that is seldom flooded.

The refuge was created to provide habitat for wood ducks, mallards and other waterfowl.

Seasonal flooding of the bottomland hardwood forest provides winter habitat for many species of waterfowl.

Section III: Long-range Management Strategy

Introduction

This section describes long-range management strategies for the Refuge's habitat, wildlife, and public use management and development programs. Specific goals, objectives, and strategies are detailed in the Objective Documentation Record (Section IV, page 29). Implementation will be further detailed in specific management plans.

As described in the previous section, the Refuge was established to preserve and restore wetlands and habitat for migratory birds and other wildlife. Management to enhance and restore the bottomland hardwood forest will balance development of areas for waterfowl and a diversity of wildlife. The Refuge contains approximately 15,000 acres of existing or potential bottomland hardwood habitat of which approximately 980 acres remain in pine plantations, and an additional 490 acres are naturally impounded. This Comprehensive Conservation Plan calls for restoration of pine plantations to bottomland hardwoods and moist soil units. Twenty acres will be managed as experimental green tree reservoirs, and approximately 100 acres will be managed as moist soil units that are dependent on rainfall and local runoff.

The general strategy for Refuge public use management is to provide most non-consumptive public use in Unit 2, while offering consumptive public use such as hunting on other units of the Refuge (see map, Appendix A). Public use roads and facilities and habitat management developments (such as the moist soil impoundment and green tree reservoirs) will be phased in over the 10-year planning period, contingent upon availability of funds.

General Management Strategy for Refuge Units

For management purposes, the Refuge has been administratively divided into five management units based on generally identifiable landmarks (see Unit Maps, Appendix A). The unit divisions help to describe, structure, and phase in planned developments and management activities.

Unit 1

Description: Unit 1 includes Refuge lands to the west of U.S. Highway 70/259 and contains approximately 3,000 acres. The unit is generally flat and wet, with numerous oxbows and sloughs. Holly Creek crosses the Refuge on the west side and Lukfata Creek crosses the east side of the unit. In the northwest corner of the unit, approximately 200 acres were flooded by beaver activities on Holly Creek prior to acquisition. Beaver activities that threaten hardwoods are now being curtailed by trapping and by removal of beaver dams to prevent further loss of hardwoods to permanent flooding (see Goal 1, page 29). Cypress trees dominate the areas of permanent water while bottomland hardwoods predominate in periodically flooded and unflooded areas.

Most of the unit was cut over in the late 1960s or early 1970s, but it is rapidly regenerating. Only one 10-acre tract had been converted to pine plantations. The remaining acreage is now characterized by vegetation typical of the Refuge, with the primary overstory consisting of young (20 to 30 year old) hardwood trees tolerant of saturated soil, such as willow oak, water oak, southern red oak, and sweet gum with a few hickory trees and pines in slightly higher ground. The understory includes hornbeam, hophornbeam, and holly.

A gas pipeline crosses the northwest corner of the unit, and an electric transmission line passes north and south through the center of the unit. Road access to the unit is difficult due to its isolation from public roads by privately owned land, and because there are limited legal access points. Access is blocked either by private property or by Holly Creek and Lukfata Creek. There are no passable internal roads. Due to the difficulty of access, the unit has attracted little public use.

Long-range Management Strategy: The inaccessibility of much of Unit 1 will restrict active management. When public access is acquired, Unit 1 will be open for public use, including bird watching and fishing. Hunting will be permitted in accordance with approved hunting plans. Access will be limited to areas off of U.S.Highway 70 until land acquisition permits legal access and parking for the northwestern part. Though no special public use facilities are planned for this unit at the present time, this policy may be reevaluated in the future. No vehicular access into this unit is planned, although a parking area is planned on the uplands on the north boundary when acquisition is complete.

Unit 2

Description: Unit 2 contains approximately 2,300 acres. It is bounded on the west by U.S. Highway 70/259. Yanubbee Creek generally defines the

18

eastern boundary and Yashau Creek crosses near the center. This unit is relatively accessible and contains a popular fishing area located at the confluence of the Little River and Yashau Creek.

The unit is generally flat and low and contains many oxbows and sloughs. There is considerable beaver-caused flooding in some areas each winter, which is controlled in the spring and summer to prevent loss of hardwoods (see Goal 1, page 29). A narrow area of uplands occurs in the northern part of the unit. In general, soil saturation is not as great as in Unit 1, so the unit supports more tree species that are less tolerant of saturated soil.

Some areas of this unit were logged prior to acquisition and today contain over 100 acres of pine plantations. Numerous sugar maples, hackberry, and a few walnut trees can be found along the banks of the Little River. Cypress trees occupy the areas of permanent water. Willow, southern red, white, shumard, and water oaks characterize the floodplain. The remainder of the young forest consists of sweet gum, nutmeg hickory, and other species in lesser numbers. The understory is a mix of holly, hornbeam, hophornbeam, and numerous vines.

Unit 2 contains a number of old timber haul roads that provide the best access of all of the units. One point on the northern part of the unit provides access for recreational uses. As a result, this area has traditionally received more fishing and hunting use than other units. However, the access road to the Refuge is narrow and crosses about a mile of land owned by Weyerhaeuser Company.

Long-range Management Strategy: Most public use development and some active natural resource management will occur on Unit 2. Public use development and maintenance will include a tour road, interpretive signs, a boat launch and parking area for fishing access, and a parking area and trails for wildlife observation and bird watching. Rabbit and squirrel hunting will continue to be allowed on Unit 2 for the immediate future but, due to potential conflicts with other users, all hunting on Unit 2 will be phased out as this management plan is implemented. Legal right-of-way into Unit 2 must be acquired for expanded public use, and roads must be developed and improved to provide safe and legal public access to and from the unit. Access into Unit 2 will be addressed in a road development and improvement plan (see Goal 7, page 44).

An experimental moist soil impoundment of approximately 100 acres will be established in Unit 2.

Unit 3

Description: Unit 3 includes 4,500 acres of Refuge land from Yanubbee Creek to the north-south access road into the Refuge. The unit contains slightly higher ground near its northern boundary, sloping southward to the Little River. It is crossed by Yanubbee and Terrapin Creeks, and contains a major oxbow lake, known locally as Yanubbee Lake, as well as numerous other oxbows and sloughs.

About one-third of this unit contains mature bottomland hardwood forest. However, 100 acres were converted to pine plantations that are generally of poor quality due to the wetness of the soils. Hardwood forest vegetation over the remainder of the tract is similar to that found in Unit 2.

The unit has relatively good access along a road that makes a loop through the area. Part of this road is maintained by the county and provides access to residents of two inholdings. The unit has an abundant squirrel population that provides recreational hunting.

Long-range Management Strategy: Unit 3 will be the second most actively managed area of the Refuge next to Unit 2. One of two experimental green tree reservoirs will be established in this unit. Unit 3 will be open to fishing, photography and wildlife observation, and other public uses not requiring facilities. Hunting will be permitted on this Unit in accordance with approved hunting plans. Acquisition of legal rights-of-way into Unit 3 will be addressed in a road development and improvement plan (see Goal 7, page 44) and acquired as numbers of Refuge visitors exceed historical, allowable levels. Public use of the area will be evaluated periodically to determine need for acquisition of legal rights-of-way until the road development and improvement plan is completed.

Unit 4

Description: Unit 4 contains approximately 2,300 acres of Refuge land extending from the main north-south access road, east to the Refuge boundary (approximately 2 miles west of the Mountain Fork River confluence). The area is relatively inaccessible due to lack of roads.

This unit is generally low and contains many sloughs and several oxbows. Horseshoe Lake, one of the oxbows, is heavily used by waterfowl in the winter. Prolonged flooding caused by beavers destroyed about 50 acres of timber near the east side before the land was acquired for the Refuge. To prevent further timber loss, beaver are currently being controlled and dams removed as needed (see Goal 1, page 29).

Although much of it has been cut over, Unit 4 still contains some of the finest quality bottomland hardwoods remaining on the Refuge, including some small tracts of relatively old timber along the river. Nearly 100 acres were converted to pine plantations prior to acquisition. Vegetation is similar to that found in Units 2 and 3.

Although there is road access to Unit 4 at three locations, all the roads cross privately owned land. This may limit the volume of public access to historical levels unless the Service can acquire additional rights-of-way.

Long-range Management Strategy: Unit 4 will have minimal development. One experimental green tree reservoir of about 10 acres is planned for this unit. Roads will be improved and parking pull-outs developed if needed to accommodate increasing visitation. Access will be evaluated periodically. Unit 4 will be open to hunting in accordance with approved hunting plans

Unit 5

Description: Unit 5 is the easternmost Refuge unit and is not contiguous with the remainder of the Refuge. Located east of the Mountain Fork River, approximately 2 miles from the main body of the Refuge, this unit extends from the Mountain Fork River east, nearly to Highway 24 south of Eagletown. The area is accessible by public road. This unit encompasses approximately 2,900 acres.

Crooked Creek flows through the middle of the unit into Forked Lake, a natural lake that then empties into the Mountain Fork River. The area is generally low, although there are several small sections of slightly higher ground to the south of the Little River that are within the boundary of the Refuge. Beaver have been very active in this unit, flooding many acres, and control measures to prevent permanent flooding damage and damage to trees have been initiated (see Goal 1, page 29).

About half of the unit has been cut over since 1965, and there are approximately 240 acres of pine plantations in the center of the unit that apparently were planted in the late 1970s. Vegetation in the unit is similar to that found in Units 2, 3, and 4. There is an excellent stand of bottomland hardwoods in the western part of this unit.

Approximately 700 acres are located on the south side of the Little River in this unit. That part of the unit is accessible by driving across the Highway 70 bridge over the Little River and approaching it from the south, a distance of approximately 15 miles from the Refuge office in Broken Bow.

South of the Little River the land rises abruptly by nearly 100 feet with steep limestone bluffs. Habitat on these bluffs includes rather poor soils with predominantly post oaks, cedar elms, and other hardwoods.

Unit 5 has several internal roads that provide access to various parts of the unit. The best access is along County Road D4770, which passes through the Refuge to an 80-acre inholding along the Little River. The unit currently receives relatively heavy public use.

Long-range Management Strategy: Bird watching, photography, and wildlife observation will be allowed in Unit 5. Fishing will also be allowed and a primitive boat launch maintained. Hunting will be permitted on this Unit in accordance with approved hunting plans. Existing functional roads will be maintained and improved and parking areas will be developed as needed to accommodate increasing numbers of visitors.

General Habitat Management Strategies

Table III-1, below, shows the acreage of existing habitat types, and acreages proposed in this Comprehensive Conservation Plan. The specific locations of developments will be evaluated and determined in a separate habitat management plan.

TABLE III-1. Proposed Changes in Habitat Acreage.

Existing Habitat		Proposed Habitat		Total Change
Acres	Types of Habitat	Acres	Types of Habitat	Acres
490	Natural impoundments*	490	Natural Impoundments*	No change
85	Rivers	85	Rivers	No change
0	Moist soil impoundments	100	Moist soil impoundments	+ 100
13,413	Bottomland hardwoods	14,285	Bottomland hardwoods (includes 20 as green tree reservoirs)	+ 872
980	Pine plantation	0	Pine plantation	- 980
0	Public use and administration facilities**	5	Public use and administration facilities**	+ 5
32	Access roads	34.2	Access roads	+ 2.2
0	Trails	0.8	Trails	+ 0.8
Total 15,000		Total 15,000		

* Permanent impoundments (oxbows, sloughs, and beaver dams) remaining during dry seasons.
** Acres covered by buildings, parking areas, landscaping, etc.

The primary objective for habitat management is conservation and enhancement of bottomland hardwood habitat for the benefit of wintering waterfowl and other migratory birds. A bottomland hardwood ecosystem depends on seasonal flooding, but the natural flooding regime of the Little

River has been disrupted by flood control dams and other human-induced factors. Pine Creek and Broken Bow Dams above the Refuge, and DeQueen, Dierks, Gillham, and Millwood Dams below the Refuge greatly reduce the chance of inundation of the river floodplain during most years. Over the course of years, the change in hydrology resulting from flood control activities may alter the bottomland hardwood ecosystem. Experimental habitat manipulations, such as green tree reservoir management, will be evaluated to determine their effectiveness in maintaining bottomland hardwoods on the Refuge.

Human-related threats to Refuge habitat include reduction in water quality from watershed erosion, and water pollution from pesticides, industrial wastes, effluent from sewage treatment, and poultry and livestock production and processing facilities. Refuge management will focus on supporting the quality of Refuge habitats with on-site measures described below, and will work with other publics and private interests to influence off-site factors affecting the Refuge.

Timber Management Strategy

No commercial timber harvest or firewood cutting programs on the Refuge are planned except as may be needed to facilitate conversion of pine plantations back to bottomland hardwoods. No grazing is planned on the Refuge because no wildlife benefits from grazing in the forested areas of the Refuge are anticipated. Specific forest habitats will be managed as described below.

Pine Plantations: Existing pine plantations will be cut when mature and allowed to regenerate into the bottomland hardwoods association.

Bottomland Hardwoods: Bottomland hardwoods are a climax community, but the oldest bottomland hardwoods in the area are only about 70 years old. These areas will be maintained for the benefit of wildlife. The Refuge will ensure proper flooding in small areas via construction and operation of green tree reservoirs as well as other means.

Wetlands Management Strategy

Rivers and Streams: Little River borders the southern edge of the Refuge, and Mountain Fork River flows along the western border of Unit 5. Several streams feeding into these rivers flow through the Refuge. No manipulations of these waters are foreseen. Water from rainfall will be used for the experimental green tree reservoirs.

Standing Water: Naturally formed, open bodies of standing water on the Refuge include oxbow lakes and beaver ponds. During periods of flooding, open water extends into the forested and cut-over areas. These impoundments are important as waterfowl roosting and feeding sites. They are also important for other wildlife such as raccoons, herons, egrets, and other migratory birds. These areas increase the natural diversity of the Refuge and will be maintained.

Additional impoundments are planned in Units 2, 3, and 4. An experimental moist soil impoundment (open, shallow, flooded area) is planned for Unit 2 to provide aquatic foods (invertebrates and seed and tuber producing annual plants) for waterfowl. Experimental impoundments for green tree reservoirs are planned for Units 3 and 4, of approximately 10 acres each. The impoundments will rely primarily on rainfall and local runoff, and will be evaluated for their value and effectiveness. If effective, consideration will be given to construction of additional impoundments.

Dams resulting from beaver activity during the fall and winter will be removed in the spring and summer to prevent destruction of hardwood forest species and interference with regeneration in recovering areas.

Grasslands Management Strategy

No natural grasslands occur on the Refuge. Within the approved Refuge boundary, however, there are several grassland areas that have been used for haying and grazing in the past. If acquired, these areas will be evaluated to determine the relative benefits of managing them as open areas for small migratory birds and other wildlife, such as deer and turkey, or allowing them to regenerate into bottomland hardwood species.

Wildlife Management Strategy

Management to increase, conserve, or control wildlife populations involves both habitat management, as previously explained, and activities relating directly to the animal populations, such as providing nest structures. Management strategies for individual species or group of species are described in detail in the Objective Documentation Record (see Section IV, page 29), following this Long-range Management Strategy.

Endangered and Threatened Species: One endangered species (Ouachita rock pocketbook mussel) and two species classified as threatened (bald eagle and American alligator) are known to occur on the Refuge. There is potential to enhance populations of these species through habitat protection and management. Management for these species will include monitoring populations on the Refuge and protection of habitat from degradation and harm by human activities.

Management programs for other wildlife will have either positive or neutral impacts on endangered and threatened species. Habitat management activities described previously, as well as in the Objective Documentation Record section, should favor listed species.

Waterfowl: The emphasis for Refuge management will be on waterfowl, with specific emphasis on mallards and wood ducks. The objective is to increase the numbers of waterfowl using the Refuge. Moist soil impoundments and green tree reservoirs will enhance habitat for waterfowl. Protection is an important consideration in increasing the number of waterfowl wintering on the Refuge. Enforcement of regulations to control illegal harvest and disturbance will be emphasized. The wood duck is the only waterfowl species known to nest in the area; implementation of a nest box program should increase their population on the Refuge.

Other Migratory Birds: A priority for Refuge management is to provide habitat for migratory birds other than waterfowl. Management for migratory birds, including shorebirds, raptors, marsh and waterbirds, and songbirds, is one purpose for which the Refuge was established. Recent emphasis has been placed on management for neotropical migratory birds. The goal for these species is to increase diversity and abundance, and management will focus on protection and enhancement of existing, natural habitat. Habitat developments aimed primarily at mallards and wood ducks will benefit many of these species, and protection of nesting and roosting areas will enhance migratory bird species numbers and diversity.

Other Wildlife: The final wildlife priority includes management for all other Refuge wildlife. The objective for these species, including birds, mammals, reptiles, amphibians, etc., is natural abundance and diversity. Management for these animals will include protection, habitat enhancement, and population monitoring.

In some instances, implementation of animal control measures may be needed to prevent conflicts with other objectives. For example, beavers build dams that permanently flood and kill trees in bottomland hardwood areas, conflicting with the Refuge's goal to restore the bottomland forest. Beaver population management and removal of beaver dams will be periodically necessary due to high population levels on the Refuge (see Goal 1, page 29).

Public Use Management Strategy

The National Wildlife Refuge System Improvement Act of 1997 recognizes six wildlife-dependent public uses, including hunting, fishing, wildlife observation and photography, and environmental education and interpretation that are to be given priority on refuges when determined to be compatible.[13] All units of the Refuge will be open for various public use activities, except during periods when flooding makes them inaccessible or use conflicts with other public uses or the needs of wildlife. Public use facilities will be developed over the 10-year planning horizon. Refuge staff will monitor public use of the Refuge and the adequacy of facilities to accommodate the level of use. Public use will be regulated to ensure that no significant environmental degradation or conflicts with wildlife objectives occur.

Volunteer help can augment the Refuge's interpretive and recreational programs. Volunteers may be used at the Refuge to enhance public use programs such as guided tours, provide help and information to visitors, assist in the operation of the visitor center, and serve in other capacities. The Refuge will develop a Volunteer Management Plan that outlines how volunteers will be recruited and trained, as well as what activities might involve volunteers.

Interpretation: Interpretation of the role of humans in the natural environment is a top priority public use objective of the Refuge. There are numerous interpretative opportunities on the Refuge.

An interpretive program will be designed in conjunction with development of interpretive facilities, including a visitor contact station, tour route, and interpretive trails. Primary interpretive themes will include: The mission of the National Wildlife Refuge System, the purposes for which the Refuge was established, and the values of bottomland hardwood forests and wetlands and their importance to waterfowl, other wildlife species, and people.

An auto-tour route will be constructed in Unit 2, using an existing road print (now partly overgrown and subject to flooding in places). Foot trails to wildlife observation points will also be constructed in Unit 2. Interpretive signs will be provided along the tour route and at strategic points along the foot trails. A Refuge headquarters and visitor contact station will be constructed and will serve as the focal point for the interpretive program.

---

[13] See footnote 8 for a definition of "compatible."

Recreation: The Refuge will offer a variety of recreational programs including wildlife observation, fishing, hunting, and hiking. These activities will center around wildlife and its enjoyment. A public use management plan will be prepared to ensure an appropriate level of development.

The times and locations of all activities, including hunting, will be designed so that there will be no major long-term impacts on waterfowl or other wildlife populations.

Three boat launches for wildlife observation and boat fishing are planned along the Little River. Parking areas for wildlife observation, hikers, boat launches, and bank anglers will be provided.

Hunting will be monitored to evaluate impacts on wildlife populations and ensure safety. All hunting will be phased out on Unit 2, but the remaining 80 percent of the Refuge will be open to hunting under Refuge regulations. Species which will be hunted on the Refuge are deer, turkey, rabbit, squirrel, raccoons, and ducks.

Most of the Refuge will be open for wildlife observation and hiking. Some areas may be closed for management purposes, particularly during special hunting seasons and in winter when visitation is low and waterfowl are more susceptible to disturbance. Designated Refuge roads will be open to the public to provide access for recreation, although seasonal closures may be necessary for management purposes.

Administrative Management Strategy

Cultural Resources: Preservation of the Refuge's cultural resources requires locating and evaluating archeological and historic sites. No formal archeological survey has been conducted on the Refuge or any of the lands proposed for addition to the Refuge. Currently, the archeological records (resulting from partial, nonsystematic surveys) indicate 19 known sites on Refuge lands (site record file: Oklahoma Archeological Survey). It is believed that past land use practices have disturbed, altered, or destroyed all these sites.

Protection of archeological, paleontological, and historical sites will be provided by Refuge personnel, through enforcement of the Archeological Resources Protection Act, the National Historic Preservation Act, and Refuge regulations. Guidance for cultural resources management and enforcement is provided by the Service's Cultural Resources Management Handbook and section 5RM 16 of the Refuge Manual. Paleontological resources are protected, along with all other Refuge natural resources, by the Antiquities Act of 1906 and resultant regulations and management documents (43 CFR 3, 310 DM 7, and the Service's Management Plan).

Research and Investigations: The Service may provide logistical and financial support for research and field study projects pertinent to Refuge management programs. Investigations that are compatible with the purposes of the Refuge and supportive of Refuge goals and objectives will be permitted.

Mineral, Oil, and Gas Resources and Economic Uses: There are currently no oil or gas wells and no mineral extraction occurring on the Refuge, and none anticipated in the immediate future. However, all mineral rights to Refuge lands are reserved by prior owners, making future development of mineral resources possible on the Refuge. Should such development occur, the Refuge Manager will work with project representatives to ensure that required roads, facilities, and surface activities are designed to minimize impacts on Refuge wildlife and habitat and that appropriate mitigation actions are taken. The Refuge Manager will monitor activities as they develop.

No other economic uses of the Refuge are anticipated.

Staffing Pattern: Current staffing of the Refuge is as follows:

Refuge Manager	GS-12
Office Assistant	GS-06
Refuge Operations Specialist	GS-11
Public Outreach Specialist	GS-11

The development and direction of the Refuge over the next ten years, based on this Comprehensive Conservation Plan, will require two additional staff in permanent full-time positions. These positions will be phased in as needed to implement the plan, contingent upon availability of funds. They are detailed in the following section.

Section IV: Objective
Documentation Record

➡️ **Goal 1:** The protection, restoration, and maintenance of the bottomland hardwood forest plant community.

✳ **Objective:** Restore pine plantations to bottomland hardwood habitat (980 acres).

Current Status: In the years prior to acquisition, some lands now within the Refuge were cleared of bottomland hardwood timber and converted to pine plantations.

Rationale for Objective: Pine plantations do not provide the benefits for waterfowl and other wildlife that are provided by oak, hickory, and other bottomland hardwood species. Restoration of these areas by conversion to bottomland hardwood species will enhance the area for wildlife species associated with bottomland hardwoods. Much of the area surrounding the refuge is in privately owned pine plantations.

Strategies for Accomplishing Objective:

- Conduct research to determine the most cost-effective, environmentally beneficial method for restoring bottomland hardwood species to areas now in pine plantations.

- Contract for thinning or removal of pines in plantations beginning in 2000. Encourage hardwood regeneration in pine understory until final cuts are made to release hardwoods.

- If natural regeneration is too slow, replant the area using locally produced seedlings, acorns, and/or seeds of endemic species.

- Evaluate potential benefits of controlled cold weather burning for accelerating hardwood regeneration.

✳ Objective: **Manage beaver populations to control damage to bottomland hardwood habitat resulting from permanent flooding.**

Current Status: Beavers have caused extensive flooding throughout the Refuge by construction of dams that inhibit water flow. At the time the Refuge was established, about 250 acres were already flooded due to beaver activity. Many trees in those areas are now dead. Prior to acquisition of the Refuge, beaver populations had increased dramatically concurrent with the drop in fur prices and related trapping. Permanent flooding caused by beaver dam construction ultimately kills trees, unlike the periodic, short-term flooding that naturally occurs with rainfall and runoff and to which bottomland hardwood species are adapted. Tree roots must be able to obtain oxygen in the soil, and permanent water around the roots, such as that created by beaver dams, prevents the uptake of oxygen and causes trees to die within about 2 years. In addition, beavers' feeding habits (they chew the bark of trees and shrubs) may kill trees.

Beavers have created problems in the local area as well as on the Refuge, building dams and flooding the many creeks and ponds that offer suitable habitat. As a result, a full-time beaver trapper has been hired by the county to remove nuisance beavers from off-Refuge areas where they plug culverts and cause flooding, gnaw down and/or flood and kill valuable timber resources, and burrow into earthen dams in ponds.

There is a strong public perception that the Refuge is serving as a source for beavers that invade private lands and cause destruction of plantations and other private property. Reproduction occurring in areas that harbor beavers results in increased populations in surrounding areas, since younger beavers generally are driven from established territory of adults and must seek new areas in which to establish their own territories.

Rationale for Objective: The major problem resulting from beaver activities is flooding of bottomland hardwoods and destruction of trees that provide food and habitat to wildlife. Permitting beaver activities that cause serious destruction of native trees is counterproductive to the Refuge's efforts to preserve and restore bottomland hardwoods. Uncontrolled beaver activity will result in additional acres being permanently flooded and the hardwood trees in the flooded areas being destroyed. The public perception that the Refuge is serving as a source for problem beavers that cause damage to neighboring private land also makes a control program important.

Beaver activities can provide some benefits to the Refuge and are an important part of the ecosystem. Short-term beaver dam construction on the Refuge can benefit wildlife since it results in flooding of the bottomlands in areas where acorns and other foods then become accessible

30

to waterfowl. Such flooding causes no harm during the winter when trees are dormant. When trees break dormancy in early spring, however, the water must be quickly removed before damage occurs from lack of oxygen to tree roots. A program of beaver control will minimize damage and destruction to trees and other plants on the Refuge and on adjacent private lands, and assist in accomplishing Refuge objectives and maintaining good neighbor relations.

Beavers often build dams in remote areas that are extremely difficult or impossible to access with heavy equipment. Explosives can be used effectively to remove dams without physically harming beavers. However, beavers usually rebuild the dams within 2 days. Therefore, use of explosives alone is not an effective method of damage control. If dams are continually destroyed, beavers may move to another location, possibly on surrounding private property where they cause problems for Refuge neighbors and result in poor Refuge/neighbor relations. Therefore, a combination of dam destruction with explosives and beaver removal provides the most effective control.

Strategies for Accomplishing Objective:

- During late winter each year, locate beaver dams on the Refuge and destroy them using explosives. If beavers start to rebuild the dams, remove beaver by shooting or underwater trapping.

- Control beaver populations through shooting or underwater trapping as needed to constrain their movement onto lands neighboring the Refuge and minimize damage to bottomland hardwoods.

- Monitor the effects of beaver flooding on Refuge trees and waterfowl populations through periodic surveillance.

✱ Objective: **Maintain a healthy, biologically diverse ecosystem that provides wildlife benefits unique to bottomland hardwood forests.**

Current Status: Traditional uses of land along the Little River have been varied. Many landowners manage their land for pastures and hayfields. Most of the land in the county is owned by large timber companies whose primary objective is to grow pine timber in the most economical manner. This economic incentive has resulted in conversion of much hardwood forest acreage to pine plantations, with displacement of species associated with the hardwood ecosystem.

The U.S. Forest Service owns a large amount of land in the county that is primarily managed for timber production (both pines and hardwoods), in which bottomland areas are protected. Biological diversity is maintained through selective cutting to maintain uneven-aged stands of mixed hardwoods and pines.

Rationale for Objective: Migratory bird species have steadily lost bottomland hardwood habitat as clearing for agricultural and urban development has progressed. Refuge lands provide an opportunity to restore the complexity and rich wildlife habitat that the bottomland hardwood forest is capable of providing.

Strategies for Accomplishing Objectives:

- Restore habitat to bottomland hardwood forest through natural regeneration, planting, or seeding as appropriate.

- Monitor vegetation to determine changes that might adversely affect the ecosystem.

- Protect habitats that harbor species of special significance through restricting public access as needed.

- When opportunities arise, cooperate with other landowners in efforts to protect the watershed.

➡ Goal 2: The restoration of native threatened and endangered species through optimum use of Refuge lands.

✳ Objective: Maintain and, if possible, double the numbers of bald eagles currently using the Refuge.

Current Status: The Little River and its oxbow lakes traditionally have supported a wintering population of bald eagles. Declines and recoveries of bald eagles in the Little River area reflect national trends. During the months of December, January, and February, bald eagle use of the Refuge varies from one to five birds.

Rationale for Objective: Bald eagles use wetland habitats such as those provided by the Refuge. Development of impoundments, plus the added protection offered by the Refuge, should result in a small increase in bald eagle usage. The Refuge could accommodate more eagles than anticipated by the objective. However, it is assumed that low numbers in the flyway and more attractive lake and riparian habitat outside the area of the Refuge will result in continued low numbers of wintering eagles on the Refuge.

Strategies for Accomplishing Objective:

- Provide increased protection for bald eagles.

- Develop green tree reservoirs (see Strategies under Goal 3, page 35) to be usable by bald eagles as well as other species.

- Monitor the quality of all waters on the Refuge.

- Inform the public regarding the presence and status of bald eagles through news releases, leaflets, and educational materials.

* Objective: Protect and maintain other listed and candidate species that are known to inhabit the Refuge.

Current Status: Listed species that are known to occur on the Refuge include the endangered Ouachita rock pocketbook mussel and the threatened American alligator and American bald eagle.

The American alligator is classified as threatened. The Refuge represents the northwest extreme of its range and it is rare in the area with fewer than 100 individuals estimated on the Refuge. American alligators inhabit areas where disturbance is minimized. The Little and Mountain Fork Rivers and associated oxbows and sloughs provide suitable habitat for this species.

The Ouachita rock pocketbook mussel was found in very small numbers in riffle areas in the Little River during a recent search by the Oklahoma Natural Heritage Inventory.

Rationale for Objective: Listed species require protection under provisions of the Endangered Species Act. Thus, the American alligator and Ouachita rock pocketbook mussel must be protected on the Refuge. No trade-offs of lower priority objectives are expected, as management for these species involves little, if any, habitat alteration.

Strategies for Accomplishing Objectives:

- Identify habitat used by each listed species. Monitor population levels.

- Protect and restore habitat to maintain and increase numbers, and restrict human access to habitat areas to enhance survival potential and increase populations.

- Monitor quality of Refuge waters and work cooperatively with other local interests within the area of ecological concern to address any problems identified.

* Objective: Determine if the listed species in Table IV-1 (see below) occur on the Refuge, and if so, protect and maintain their populations.

TABLE IV-1. Endangered and Threatened Species that may be found on the Refuge.

Species	Scientific Name	Status
Birds Red-cockaded Woodpecker Peregrine Falcon	*Picoides borealis* *Falco peregrinus*	Endangered Threatened
Insects American burying beetle	*Nicrophorus Americanus*	Endangered

Current Status: These listed species are known to occur in southeast Oklahoma and the general area of the Refuge. None are known to occur on the Refuge, and it does not appear that suitable habitats exist on the Refuge for these species.

Rationale for Objective: Listed species require protection under provisions of the Endangered Species Act and receive special consideration in management programs. Protection and management of listed species on the Refuge will aid in their recovery.

Strategies for Accomplishing Objective:

- Review literature to determine habitat needs of listed species potentially occurring on the Refuge and determine habitat suitability.

- Conduct surveys for listed species and compile location and population data for any species found.

- Manage or, if feasible, develop suitable habitat on the Refuge for these species.

➡ **Goal 3:** The protection and enhancement of habitat for migratory bird use.

✳ **Objective:** Enhance Refuge habitat to accommodate 100,000 mallard and 150,000 wood duck use days per year by the year 2005.

Current Status: Wintering mallards and wood ducks in southeastern Oklahoma traditionally have been associated with bottomland hardwood habitats. No historical records are available, but it is presumed that use of the Refuge bottomland varied with both flyway and weather trends prior to establishment of the Refuge in 1987. The current level of mallard use is approximately 70,000 use days, and wood duck use is also approximately 70,000 use days. Competition from free roaming swine for mast (nuts from forest trees) may adversely affect waterfowl numbers and may have restricted use in the past. Resident wood duck populations have also been limited by predation and lack of suitable tree cavities for nesting.

Rationale for Objective: The purposes of the Refuge include preservation of wetlands for migratory waterfowl use. Mallards and wood ducks have been identified as key waterfowl species that depend on bottomland hardwood forest wetlands. Destruction of waterfowl wintering habitat in southeastern Oklahoma and adjacent states as a result of land use practices may result in concentration of the remaining mallard and wood duck populations into shrinking remnants of suitable habitat.

McCurtain County lost approximately 195,000 acres of bottomland hardwood habitat, or 82 percent of its original resource, between 1830 and 1982. Approximately 42,000 acres of bottomland hardwood habitat remained in 1982. At the current rate of loss, only 19,000 acres will remain by the year 2040. At that time, the Refuge would contain almost 80 percent of the remaining bottomland hardwood habitat within the county.

The steady loss of waterfowl habitat in the county will make the Refuge increasingly valuable for mallards and wood ducks, and Refuge populations will grow accordingly. The major limiting factor to Refuge mallard and wood duck populations will be the relative numbers of these waterfowl in this part of the flyway.

Active management to improve the quality of habitat on the Refuge, through providing wood duck nesting boxes and establishing green tree reservoirs, should result in increases in wintering and resident mallards and wood ducks, as well as other waterfowl species, and should guarantee that some areas will have optimum habitat conditions each year for waterfowl pair bonding and late winter conditioning.

Strategies for Accomplishing Objective:

- Protect bottomland hardwood habitat on the Refuge.

- Convert 20 acres to green tree reservoirs to provide additional food resources for waterfowl in 2000. The green tree reservoirs will be monitored to assess impacts on tree species composition, waterfowl usage, and other factors.

- Protect roosting and feeding areas from disturbance.

- Control and remove livestock (cattle and swine) that stray onto the Refuge and that may compete with waterfowl for food and interfere with hardwood regeneration.

- If pine plantations do not regenerate to hardwood species satisfactorily after cutting, plant willow oak, water oak, southern red oak, various hickories, green ash, and other native species which produce quality food for mallards and wood ducks.

- Install 50 wood duck nest boxes in 2000 and evaluate usage in 2002 to determine additional need.

- Protect trees containing cavities that may be used by wood ducks for nesting.

- Construct an experimental 100 acre moist soil impoundment in Unit 2.

* Objective: Enhance Refuge habitat to accommodate approximately 40,000 use days for gadwall, wigeon, green-winged teal, and other waterfowl species.

Current Status: Several species of waterfowl other than mallards and wood ducks use the Refuge during migration and wintering. Puddle duck species such as green-winged teal, gadwall, and wigeon may be found using Refuge oxbow lakes and streams, particularly during winter. These species stop to rest and feed on Refuge impoundments. No historical records are available, but it is presumed that use has varied with flyway trends. Protection offered since establishment of the Refuge has resulted in increases in numbers of these species.

Rationale for Objective: The Service has responsibility for protection and perpetuation of waterfowl under treaties with Canada and Mexico. These responsibilities are identified both in the specified goals of the National Wildlife Refuge System and in the Refuge purpose statement.

Loss of wetlands in the area has displaced waterfowl into areas where habitat remains. Puddle ducks generally prefer large, shallow, flooded impoundments. In the spring, diving ducks may also use larger impoundments in small numbers. Providing quality habitat for all species of waterfowl will enhance their populations and help to offset habitat loss elsewhere.

Strategies for Accomplishing Objective:

- Protect nesting and wintering waterfowl.

- Design hunting programs to minimize waterfowl disturbance.

- Provide a diversity of quality wetland habitats to accommodate a diversity of waterfowl species.

- Manage waterfowl hunting to sustain healthy populations.

* Objective: **Maintain and develop habitat to support the natural diversity of neotropical and other nongame bird species native to the bottomland hardwood forest.**

Current Status: The bottomland hardwood forest of the Refuge contains a natural diversity of habitats that attract numerous species of migratory birds in addition to waterfowl. The restoration and maintenance of the bottomland hardwood forest on the Refuge will help support and perpetuate populations of many species of songbirds and other migratory birds.

Rationale for Objective: The Service has responsibility for protection and perpetuation of migratory birds under treaties with both Canada and Mexico. That responsibility is reflected both in the specified goals of the National Wildlife Refuge System and in the Refuge purpose statements. Protection and perpetuation of neotropical birds is, therefore, a mandated function of the Refuge.

Strategies for Accomplishing Objective:

- Restore native bottomland hardwood habitat.

- In 1999, design the two 10-acre experimental green tree reservoirs planned for Units 3 and 4 in a manner that will benefit a variety of species in addition to waterfowl, including sandpipers, rails, herons, egrets, hawks, neotropical migratory birds, etc. Construct in 2000, funds permitting.

- Protect nesting migratory birds from disturbance during the months of February through June by controlling access to heron and egret rookeries and other critical nesting, resting, and feeding areas.

- Encourage additional wildlife diversity through water level manipulation in managed impoundments (moist soil management and green tree reservoirs).

- Monitor Refuge water quality.

- Monitor population levels of migratory birds to determine the success of various management techniques.

➡ Goal 4: **The protection and enhancement of Refuge habitat to sustain healthy populations of native fish and wildlife species.**

* Objective: **Ensure that water quality on the Refuge is maintained and improved to provide optimal habitat for fish and other species.**

Current Status: Water resources on the Refuge derive from two rivers, Little and Mountain Fork, and several creeks, including Holly, Lukfata, Yashau, Yanubbee, Terrapin, and Crooked. There are a diverse number of potential pollution sources along these waterways, including sewage effluent, runoff from timber and farming operations, chicken production and processing industry, a sawmill, and a fiberboard plant. Two dams on the rivers affect water temperatures and hydrology. The Oklahoma Department of Health regularly monitors water quality in several areas in and near the Refuge, and water quality studies are being conducted periodically by the U.S. Fish and Wildlife Service's Oklahoma Ecological Services Field Office in Tulsa and other agencies.

Rationale for Objective: Clean water is essential to the health of wetland wildlife species. Although the water in the Little River has been determined to be of high quality, the potential exists for contamination and deterioration of water quality from both point and nonpoint sources. Changes in water flow patterns due to dam construction upstream also can affect the deposition of sediments, turbidity, and other water quality factors.

Strategies for Accomplishing Objective:

- In 2001, evaluate the existing water monitoring program[14] and modify it as appropriate to adequately determine changes in water quality over time.

- Ensure that all new artificial constructions on the Refuge (such as construction of impoundments or development of roads for public use), as well as improvements of existing roads, are designed to minimize interference with the natural movement of water.

- Work cooperatively with other local interests within the area of ecological concern to address problems that may be identified.

✷ Objective: **Manage the Refuge white-tailed deer herd to maintain a stable population with minimum adverse effects on Refuge habitat.**

Current Status: The diversity and quality of habitat on the Refuge has accommodated deer since the State of Oklahoma reintroduced them to the to the area in the 1960s. Factors such as poaching and habitat degradation initially resulted in a low Refuge population. The population began to increase when the Refuge was established in 1987. However, protection of deer on the Refuge from poaching and harassment will likely result in a continuing increase in deer populations, although movement of deer off of and onto the Refuge will limit Refuge populations somewhat.

Rationale for Objective: The increase in deer on the Refuge was desirable to a point. However, because there are no large predators to limit that population growth, eventually damage to Refuge vegetation could occur. Controlled hunting is an effective way to maintain deer populations at healthy levels compatible with the restoration of the bottomland forest.

---

[14] Currently being conducted by the Oklahoma Ecological Services Field Office, U.S. Fish and Wildlife Service, and the Health Department of the State of Oklahoma.

Strategies for Accomplishing Objective:

- Protect the herd from harassment by controlling illegal activity such as poaching, off-road vehicles, trespass, and running deer with hunting dogs.

- As additional Refuge lands are acquired, install boundary fencing in a manner that will minimize hazards to deer and avoid restricting their movement.

- Maintain high visibility of Refuge personnel through frequent patrols to prevent deer poaching.

- In cooperation with the Oklahoma Department of Wildlife Conservation, regulate the harvest of deer, including limiting the number of hunters and the length of hunts.

- Monitor the population to determine herd health and population trends.

- Minimize competition for food by controlling trespass livestock.

* Objective: **Maintain and enhance the natural diversity of wildlife species traditionally associated with bottomland hardwood habitats.**

Current Status: The Refuge represents an extreme northwest range of the bottomland hardwood habitat type typical of river floodplains in the southern United States. The wildlife species associated with this habitat type farther south and east are also found on the Refuge. Various habitat manipulation techniques in the years preceding establishment of the Refuge have changed much of the bottomland hardwood habitat to a more diverse system, comprised of typical bottomland hardwood habitat, regenerating cut over areas and established pine plantations. These changes have resulted in fragmentation of the bottomland hardwood habitat and reduction of species dependent on this habitat.

Rationale for Objective: Conservation of "a natural diversity and abundance of fauna and flora on Refuge lands. . ." is one of the four goals of the National Wildlife Refuge System. On the Refuge, the range of habitats found in the bottomland hardwood ecosystem will provide for a natural diversity of many species of wildlife in addition to migratory birds and game animals, including a variety of reptiles, amphibians, and mammals. This natural diversity will be supported by the restoration and maintenance of the bottomland hardwood forest community on the Refuge.

Strategies for Accomplishing Objective:

- Restore and maintain bottomland hardwood forest.

- Protect species from illegal taking and disturbance.

- Control species, such as beaver, when their activities threaten habitat of other native wildlife populations or the health or restoration of bottomland hardwood forest resources (see Goal 1, page 29).

➡ Goal 5: Compliance with historic and archeological resource protection laws and regulations.

✱ Objective: Provide full protection to Refuge archeological, paleontological, and cultural resources to prevent their inadvertent loss or destruction.

Current Status: Refer to pages 10-11 for a description of cultural resources found on the Refuge.

Rationale for Objective: To comply with the Refuge Manual and the Regional Cultural Resources Policy, refuges are required to follow established policies and procedures in the following areas: (1) refuge construction projects; (2) law enforcement; (3) visitor use; (4) special use permits--research referral; (5) special use permits--non-Service land use; (6) reporting new cultural resources; (7) reporting maintenance, stabilization, and protection needs; (8) National Register nominations; and (9) archives and collections.

Strategies for Accomplishing Objectives:

- Comply with provisions outlined in 5 RM 16 of the Refuge Manual and the 1984 Cultural Resources Management Policy Statements regarding the preservation-in-place objective.

- Coordinate with the Regional Historic Preservation Officer for assistance with cultural resource surveys and formal consultations prior to any construction that could impact known or unknown cultural resources.

41

- Provide law enforcement as needed against unauthorized removal of cultural artifacts.

- Refer all archeological research permit requests to the Regional Historic Preservation Officer.

- Consult the Regional Historic Preservation Officer regarding any cultural resource sites or objects found by or reported to Refuge personnel.

- Provide recommendations to the Regional Historic Preservation Officer for methods for stabilizing, maintaining, or protecting sites that are being impacted by natural events or human actions.

➡ Goal 6: The development of a biological information database for use in monitoring ecosystem changes and making management decisions.

✳ Objective: Map and monitor Refuge habitat types and wildlife use areas.

Current Status: There are no existing maps that show plant compositions of the various Refuge habitat types. Infrared aerial photographs of the Refuge taken in 1989 and 1994 indicate gross habitat variations. National Wetlands Inventory data and maps provide information on substrate, depth of water, gross vegetation types, etc., rather than the more detailed information on plant composition needed for effective Refuge management.

The Nature Conservancy is currently developing a Habitat Classification System that may be useful for Refuge planning and management purposes. Other systems already developed may be useful if modified for Refuge purposes.

Rationale for Objective: Because this Refuge is relatively new, little data is available for this Comprehensive Conservation Plan. This data is needed to ensure optimal management of Refuge resources. Aerial photographs and other remotely sensed information will continue to be useful in evaluating gross vegetational changes over time.

Strategies for Accomplishing Objective:

- Establish a map record of vegetational changes based on permanent transects and analysis of existing and future aerial photographs.

- Establish a habitat classification system for documenting the current habitat types within the Refuge and monitor changes.

- Map wildlife habitat on the Refuge to indicate:
    - areas preferred by wintering waterfowl,
    - areas of high wildlife use, and
    - areas that accommodate endangered and threatened species.

* Objective: **Create a computerized database of Refuge biological resources.**

Current Status: Establishment of a biological database for the Refuge has begun with production of various species lists for the Refuge including bird, reptile, amphibian, fish, mammal, and mollusk. Breeding bird databases also have been established. A list of trees is being developed (see Appendix B), and a baseline data-gathering research project on water quality in the Little River and its tributaries has been initiated.

Rationale for Objective: Monitoring of this ecosystem to determine changes will be necessary to ensure restoration and preservation of bottomland hardwood forest and wildlife values. Data are needed in order to monitor the long-term health of the Refuge's bottomland hardwoods ecosystem, identify factors influencing that health, and to evaluate the effectiveness of management techniques.

Relatively little biological data are available for the Refuge. Additional information is needed to ensure wise management of Refuge resources. Obtaining some of the information needed will require projects designed to collect baseline data and monitor habitat changes.

Strategies for Accomplishing Objective:

- Collect fish and wildlife species-related data important for making management decisions, including the following:

  - Production data for wood ducks on the Refuge.

  - The occurrence of endangered, threatened, and candidate species on the Refuge.

43

- Waterfowl use of the Refuge.

- Collect plant data for the Refuge, including species, habitats, and relative abundance.

- Establish tracts to monitor habitat and wildlife use changes.

- Encourage research activities on the Refuge that will provide resource data for future reference and use.

- Design a species database using the Fish and Wildlife Service Wildlife Inventory Database system, and incorporate data collected into this system for easy retrieval, use, and evaluation.

Goal 7: A public that: (1) enjoys and values fish and wildlife resources found on the Refuge; (2) understands events and issues related to these resources; and (3) acts to promote fish and wildlife conservation.

* Objective: Provide enhanced opportunities to view and appreciate wildlife on the Refuge.

Current Status: The Refuge currently has very little non-consumptive recreational use such as birding and hiking, due to the lack of roads, parking areas, road pull-offs and viewing stops, and trails. There are a few places suitable for parking a small number of vehicles, but most of these are dirt pull-offs and clearings adjacent to primitive boat launching sites. Old timber roads are sometimes used by visitors for walking and bird watching, but these are not currently suitable for general public use. Due to inadequate road conditions and periodic flooding, no designated auto-tour route currently exists on the Refuge.

Most of the roads leading to the Refuge cross private lands. Under existing conditions, public access at historical levels is allowed. In order to accommodate traffic above historical levels, additional legal access and right-of-way for increased traffic must be acquired and roads widened and improved. Existing roads both into and on the Refuge are narrow, in fair to poor condition, and sometimes suited only for four-wheel drive and utility vehicles.

Unit 2 offers the best opportunities for wildlife and wildlands viewing, both currently and in the long-term management plan. Consequently, this unit is the most suitable for an interpretive tour route and trails, since it will offer viewing of several habitat types, including bottomland hardwood habitat, oxbow sloughs, and a river overlook. Other units do not have the level of aesthetic appeal that Unit 2 offers.

Rationale for Objective: Although recreational use in the vicinity of the Refuge has traditionally focused on hunting and fishing, there is a growing public interest and need for bird watching opportunities, walking trails, and other non-consumptive recreational use sites and facilities. The Service has a responsibility to provide such opportunities when they can be offered without conflicting with the needs of wildlife.

People have a need to relate to wildlife and wildlife habitat. Providing opportunities for non-consumptive recreational uses will help satisfy that need. The intent of this objective is to accommodate an anticipated increase in the number of Refuge visitors wishing to observe wildlife.

Strategies for Accomplishing Objective:

- Acquire legal right-of-ways into Refuge Units and construct roads that are safe for all types of vehicles, to accommodate a slowly increasing volume of traffic into the Refuge (see next objective).

- Prepare a public use management plan.

- Design and construct a tour road for automobiles through Unit 2 on the existing road print, with pull-outs for wildlife viewing.

- Establish a parking area to accommodate 12 cars, for those who wish to explore the Refuge on foot.

- Develop walking trails for wildlife viewing.

- Improve boating access in Unit 2 for non-fishing public use as well as use by the fishing public.

✳ Objective: **Improve access into the Refuge for public and agency use.**

Current Status: Roads into Units 2, 3, and 4 are narrow and barely accommodate two-way traffic. There are no roads into Unit 1. The bulk of Refuge traffic is for fishing access. Any improvements on the Refuge that will increase traffic will require acquisition of additional right-of-ways across private land, or establishment of new roads into Refuge units. Existing roads are not wide enough to avoid potential conflicts with timber hauling vehicles during harvest periods and with and between visitors in vehicles such as motor homes, school buses, and vehicles pulling large camping trailers.

Rationale for Objective: It is not realistic to believe that public interest in the use of the Refuge for recreation will remain static into the future. The current trends in increasing interest in visiting public lands will probably continue, and it is just a matter of time before visitation to the Refuge increases. In addition, if goals and objectives identified in this Comprehensive Conservation Plan are achieved, an increase in public use of the Refuge is likely.

It will be necessary to acquire right-of-ways sufficient to improve road access into the Refuge, or to construct an additional road or roads, to provide access into Refuge units. Public access to the Refuge should not be limited to those with utility and four-wheel drive vehicles. Also, current Refuge access roads are inadequate for additional traffic as well as two-way traffic involving large vehicles, including timber hauling vehicles.

Strategies for Accomplishing Objective:

- Conduct a feasibility study to identify alternative access routes into the Refuge, evaluating the potential environmental impact of each alternative.

- Prepare a road development and improvement plan for the Refuge that will address concerns regarding periodic flooding and potential conflicts with timber haul traffic, and that will meet minimum road standards appropriate for that area of Oklahoma.

- Negotiate with landowners whose land existing access roads now cross to determine road development opportunities and potential conflicts.

- Determine priorities for access acquisition and road development, and construct or improve roads accordingly.

✽ Objective: **Interpret for the public the important role of bottomland hardwoods in ensuring viable populations of migratory waterfowl in the Central Flyway.**

Current Status: There are no printed informational brochures prepared for the Refuge and no interpretive or informational signs other than boundary postings. There are no educational materials about bottomland hardwood forest values that relate to the Refuge.

Area inhabitants have traditionally interacted closely with wildlife and are knowledgeable about and interested in wildlife resources.

Rationale for Objective: There are many misconceptions in local communities regarding the functions of federal agencies, including the Service. Those misconceptions may lead to fear, distrust, and eventually to resistance to stated Refuge objectives. Strategies focusing on information and education will provide the most effective vehicle for establishing trust of the local communities and support for achievement of Refuge objectives.

Strategies for Accomplishing Objective:

- Prepare a Refuge informational brochure discussing the values of bottomland hardwoods and the role of the Refuge in preserving those values. Include in the brochure information about Refuge recreational resources.

- Provide interpretive signs along the tour road and at wildlife viewing stops.

- Provide interpretive signs on proposed trails.

- Prepare environmental education materials pertaining to bottomland hardwood forest values for use in local schools.

- Develop interpretive displays concerning bottomland hardwood forest values and the role of the Refuge in preserving those values, for use in schools and other public places.

✻ Objective: Develop a public outreach program.

Current Status: Due to limited staffing, communication with local communities to promote benefits offered by the Refuge has been very limited, and there is currently no formal outreach program.

Rationale for Objective: Although local people are knowledgeable regarding wildlife and nature, and are aware of hunting and fishing opportunities on the Refuge, they are not yet aware of other opportunities for recreation and education that the Refuge offers.

Strategies for Accomplishing Objective:

- Seek assistance of Regional Office, Oklahoma Ecological Services Field Office, and other Refuge outreach personnel to develop a public outreach strategy. Include in the strategy the following elements:

- Assess public outreach needs, particularly those that are related to existing or potential issues.

- Identify goals and messages of the public outreach strategy.

- Identify target audiences and potential public involvement.

- Develop audience-specific messages and programs.

- Identify outreach tools.

- Design a time frame for implementation and evaluation.

- Provide public outreach training to Refuge staff.

* Objective: **Offer a program in which the services of volunteers can be incorporated into the Refuge operations and maintenance programs.**

Current Status: There is no volunteer program at present. Several people have expressed interest in doing volunteer work on the Refuge during the past few years, and there is potential for an excellent volunteer program.

Rationale for Objective: People who work on a refuge understand the need for, and become advocates for the refuge, developing community-based support. Visitors to the refuge benefit from the work of volunteers including personal contacts with individuals who can provide information about the refuge and the surrounding area. Volunteers can complete projects that otherwise would require use of refuge funds, freeing those funds for use in enhancing the refuge for both wildlife and visitors.

Strategies for Accomplishing Objective:

- Incorporate a volunteer program into the Refuge program.

- Develop public use facilities and programs.

- Develop a network of "Friends of the Refuge."

➡️ **Goal 8:** Expanded recreational hunting and fishing programs.

✳ **Objective:** Plan a special annual waterfowl hunt on the Refuge.

Current Status: Prior to establishment of the Refuge in 1987, waterfowl were hunted intensively on their roosts, depleting their numbers and resulting in relatively low populations. Since the establishment of the Refuge, no waterfowl hunting was allowed prior to 1997 and duck populations have recovered. A special waterfowl hunt was first conducted in fall 1997. This hunt has been designed to control harvest and minimize disturbance.

Rationale for Objective: Hunting is one of the six priority public uses on National Wildlife Refuges. Duck hunting has been determined to be a compatible activity.[15] Most of the quality wetlands remaining in the area are now included in the Refuge, and many duck hunters have few other places to hunt.

Strategies for Accomplishing Objective:

- Evaluate Refuge lands to determine which areas are most suitable for a public waterfowl hunt.

- Conduct regular censuses of waterfowl on the refuge to determine population and area use trends.

- Cooperate with the state in conducting waterfowl hunting on the Refuge.

- Evaluate the impacts of the hunting program and modify it as needed to ensure no adverse long-term impact on waterfowl populations and Refuge habitat. Conduct bag checks and waterfowl census to determine population trends and their management implications.

✳ **Objective:** Provide squirrel and rabbit hunting on the Refuge.

Current Status: Squirrel and rabbit hunting in bottomland hardwood habitat is a tradition in the area of the Refuge. Conversion of hardwood forests in

---

[15] See footnote 8 for a definition of compatibility. A compatibility determination for waterfowl hunting was made in conjunction with preparation of the Refuge Waterfowl Management Plan.

the area to pine plantations unsuitable for squirrels has resulted in a greater demand for squirrel hunting on the Refuge where hardwood species and squirrels remain abundant. Squirrels and rabbits have been hunted on the Refuge since its establishment in 1987.

Rationale for Objective: Hunting is one of the six priority public uses on National Wildlife Refuges. As more hardwood areas are converted to pine plantations, squirrels will be found primarily in remaining hardwoods, concentrating hunting activity in these areas. The Refuge currently has the largest expanse of prime bottomland hardwood squirrel habitat remaining in southeastern Oklahoma. Although rabbits are not abundant on the Refuge, due to a lack of brushy habitat, their high reproductive rate makes it possible to allow hunting with no significant impact on populations.

Squirrel and rabbit hunting cause disturbance to wildlife, but most hunting occurs in the early fall, during moderate weather conditions, with little hunting activity after mid-November when waterfowl might otherwise be disturbed. Squirrel and rabbit hunting should not cause disturbance of bald eagles, waterfowl, or other sensitive species. Numbers of hunters are expected to remain within historic levels during the time period covered by this Comprehensive Conservation Plan.

Strategies for Accomplishing Objective:

- Maintain sufficient roads and parking areas to allow adequate hunter access to units.

- Monitor the number of squirrel and rabbit hunters to determine if traffic into the Refuge is increasing significantly.

- Monitor the squirrel and rabbit populations by regular censuses, hunter reports of harvest, and spot checks of hunter bags.

- Monitor impacts of hunts, and adjust program design as needed to ensure protection of Refuge habitat and other wildlife species, prevent overhunting of squirrel and rabbit populations, and avoid conflicts with other Refuge visitors.

- Although squirrel and rabbit hunting initially will be allowed in all Refuge units, they will be phased out in Unit 2 to avoid public use conflicts as other recreational activities are developed

✳ Objective: Provide archery deer hunting on the Refuge.

Current Status: Prior to establishment of the Refuge in 1987, the area was hunted intensively for deer. Due to a relatively low initial deer population and a fragmented landownership pattern, the Refuge was not opened to deer hunting until 1997. Deer had 10 years of protection on the Refuge, which permitted populations to recover.

Rationale for Objective: Hunting is one of the six priority public uses on National Wildlife Refuges. Deer populations can sustain an archery hunt and provide recreational opportunities on the Refuge.

Wildlife disturbance will result from a hunt, but its impacts will be minimized through hunt program design. Conflicts with other Refuge visitors and inholding residents will be minimized by timing of the hunts, the length of the hunts, and by prohibiting deer hunting in Unit 2.

Strategies for Accomplishing Objective:

- Cooperate with the Oklahoma Department of Wildlife Conservation to offer a deer hunt.

- Restrict Refuge hunting season to prevent conflicts with other programs.

- Deer hunting will not be allowed in Unit 2.

- Clearly post hunting areas with boundary signs.

✳ Objective: Offer a controlled spring turkey hunt on the Refuge.

Current Status: Turkeys occur in several areas of the Refuge.

Rationale for Objective: Hunting is one of the six priority public uses on National Wildlife Refuges. Turkeys have a high reproductive potential, are able to sustain a limited managed hunt, and provide recreational opportunities on the Refuge.

Wildlife disturbance will result from this hunt; however, its impacts will be minimized through hunt program design. Conflicts with other visitors and residents of inholdings will be minimized by the timing of the hunt, the length of the hunt, and by limiting the number of hunters.

Strategies for Accomplishing Objective:

- Open areas of the Refuge to archery hunting of turkeys at the same time as archery deer hunting.

- Cooperate with the Oklahoma Department of Wildlife Conservation to offer a special spring turkey hunt.

- Conduct censuses of turkeys on the Refuge.

- Post hunting areas.

- Set hunting dates to prevent conflicts with other Refuge users.

✻ Objective: **Provide raccoon hunting on the Refuge.**

Current Status: Raccoons are common on the Refuge and there are adequate numbers to support raccoon hunting. The Refuge was opened for raccoon hunting for the first time in fall 1997.

Rationale for Objective: Hunting is one of the six priority public uses on National Wildlife Refuges. Local citizens have traditionally hunted for raccoons in the bottomlands. Raccoon populations are adequate to sustain a managed hunt and provide recreational opportunities on the Refuge.

Wildlife disturbance will result from this hunt; however, its impacts will be minimized through hunt program design.

Conflicts with other visitors and residents of inholdings will be minimized by the timing of the hunt and the restricted hunting areas.

Strategies for Accomplishing Objectives:

- Cooperate with the Oklahoma Department of Wildlife Conservation to offer a raccoon hunt.

- Restrict hunting to times during fall and winter that will not conflict with other recreational activities or disrupt wintering waterfowl or nesting neotropical migrants.

- Raccoon hunting will not be permitted on Unit 2.

- Post hunting areas.

✲ Objective: Provide fishing opportunities on the Refuge.

Current Status: Bank and boat fishing has traditionally occurred on the Mountain Fork and Little Rivers, and the Refuge has been open for fishing since 1988. Fishing is allowed all year, but most occurs in late spring and summer when catfish are moving upstream to spawn.

The primary constraint to fishing on the Refuge is accessibility. Vehicle access is limited to designated roads. Primitive boat launches are provided at several locations on Refuge Units 2, 3, 4, and 5.

Rationale for Objective: Hunting is one of the six priority public uses on National Wildlife Refuges Local demand for fishing along the Little River and on the Refuge is high. Due to the seasonal nature of fishing, occurring primarily during late spring and summer, there is little conflict with wildlife activities.

Strategies for Accomplishing Objective:

● Improve access roads to fishing areas.

● Evaluate parking needs adjacent to popular fishing areas, and determine need for improvement and/or expansion.

● Construct bank fishing access points to expand fishing opportunities to a greater number of visitors.

● Improve existing boat launch facilities to control erosion.

● Provide universally designed access.

➡ **Goal 9: Efficient administration that supports accomplishment of Refuge objectives.**

✲ Objective: Complete step-down plans for implementation of objectives and strategies identified in this Comprehensive Conservation Plan.

Current Status: The Refuge Upland Game Hunting and Fishing Management Plan was completed in 1988. Hunting plans for deer, raccoon, turkey, and waterfowl were prepared in FY 1997. The Refuge currently coordinates with the State in areawide waterfowl planning. The following plans are still needed (listed in priority order with estimated year by which the plans will be submitted for approval):

    (1) Animal Control Plan - 1999
    (2) Road Development and Improvement Plan - 1999
    (3) Safety Plan - 1999
    (4) Fire Management Plan - 1999
    (5) Public Use Management Plan- 1999
    (6) Habitat Management Plan - 2000
    (7) Wildlife Inventory Plan - 2000
    (8) Law Enforcement Plan - 2001
    (9) Disease Prevention and Control Plan - 2001

Rationale for Objective: All activities on the Refuge must (a) meet requirements of the National Environmental Policy Act and (b) be compatible with the primary purposes for which the Refuge was established. As a result, plans must be prepared for all Refuge management programs.

✻ Objective: **Increase Refuge staff to meet minimal requirements for implementation of Refuge objectives and strategies in this Comprehensive Conservation Plan.**

Current Status:

Refuge Manager	GS-12
Refuge Operations Specialist	GS-11
Public Outreach Specialist	GS-11
Office Assistant	GS-06

Rationale for Objective: Current staffing patterns are inadequate to meet the requirements of expanded activity on the Refuge. While full staffing is not needed immediately, additional staffing will be necessary as improvements are made, habitat improvement programs are implemented, and public use increases.

Strategies for Accomplishing Objective: The future development and direction of the Refuge, based on this Comprehensive Conservation Plan, will require the addition of two staff in permanent full-time positions. A WG-08 equipment operator and a WG-07 maintenance worker will be needed for the additional maintenance required by construction of the visitor contact station, auto tour route, additional parking and pull-out sites, additional access roads, and additional waterfowl impoundments.

Funding permitting, the two additional positions will be added in FY 2001.

✳ **Objective:** **Construct a permanent Refuge headquarters and visitor contact station on Refuge lands.**

Current Status: The Refuge office is currently located in rented space in a shopping center in Broken Bow. It is difficult for the public to locate the office; and, because it is a considerable distance from the Refuge, the site does not permit efficient contact with Refuge visitors.

Rationale for Objective: A headquarters and visitor contact station located on the Refuge will provide the public with easy access to information and provide Refuge staff with quick accessibility in the event of problems or emergencies.

Strategies for Accomplishing Objective:

● Identify the site that best meets the needs of Refuge operations and maintenance, including the accommodation of visitors.

● Determine space needs for Refuge operations and maintenance staff and equipment.

● Identify funding needs and funding schedule.

✳ **Objective:** **Acquisition of adequate equipment and storage facilities to implement management strategies identified in this management plan.**

Current Status: The Refuge has a radio communications system that allows communication between the office and personnel in the field. It also has vehicles for use in various administration functions.

The Refuge currently has no maintenance or construction equipment (e.g., backhoe, front-end loader) except a tractor with a mower and currently relies on contracting for all equipment work.

Because the Refuge office is located in the town of Broken Bow, 6 miles from the nearest Refuge lands and about 15 miles from the farthest point on the Refuge, construction of storage facilities on the Refuge will not be practical until a headquarters/visitor contact station is built on Refuge lands.

Rationale for Objective: Radios are required for communication between the field, the office, and other personnel. This equipment suffers normal wear and tear and will require periodic replacement. Refuge staff require safe, dependable vehicles to carry out normal duties. Thus, vehicles must be replaced periodically as they wear out. Equipment is needed to maintain roads and to construct and maintain impoundments. Purchase of equipment will allow dependable scheduling of maintenance. With the purchase of equipment, a storage building will be needed, either rented in town or constructed on the Refuge.

Equipment is needed to remove debris and beaver plugs from culverts, water control structures, and streams to allow proper water management on the Refuge and prevent destruction of bottomland hardwoods resulting from beaver activities. Periodic flooding damages Refuge roads. Road maintenance equipment is needed to ensure continued access for management purposes and public use.

Strategies for Accomplishing Objectives:

- Identify current and projected Refuge equipment and storage facility needs based on management activity priorities and schedules for implementation.

- Acquire equipment as needed to meet management objective implementation requirements identified for each year.

* Objective: **Limit economic uses to those that are mandated or needed to accomplish other Refuge objectives.**

Current Status: Lands that are now, or may eventually be, part of the Refuge have historically been used primarily for timber production and livestock grazing. After purchase of the lands for inclusion in the Refuge, these practices were halted due to conflicts with the purposes for which the Refuge was established. The Refuge does not own any mineral rights on Refuge lands. No mineral extraction is currently occurring or planned.

Rationale for Objective: Economic uses that are compatible with the purposes for which the Refuge was acquired and consistent with Refuge objectives may be allowed under authority of the National Wildlife Refuge System Administration Act (see Appendix C).

Strategies for Accomplishing Objective:

- Since the Refuge does not own mineral rights to the land, exploration for and development of mineral and energy resources (i.e., gas and oil) are allowed (see 5 RM 13 of the Refuge Manual). Permits will be issued for exploration and development activities as required.

- Economic uses that will impart benefits to native wildlife, such as cutting of pine plantations, may be permitted.

- Economic uses that do not benefit Refuge habitat will not be allowed.

Unimproved roads provide access to visitors except when flooded.

Great egrets nest in trees near sloughs and other open water areas.

Cypress trees predominate in areas that are seasonally flooded and soils are wet most of the time.

Section V: Management Action Plan
Synthesis by Fiscal Year

Fiscal Year 1999

1. Acquire and/or create safe and legal rights-of-way into Refuge units.

2. Prepare an informal Refuge brochure discussing the values of bottomland hardwoods.

3. Develop interpretive displays concerning bottomland hardwood forest values for use in schools and other public places.

4. Improve access roads to fishing areas.

5. Evaluate parking needs for popular fishing areas and determine need for improvement and/or expansion.

6. Prepare management plans for (1) Animal Control, (2) Safety, (3) Fire Management, and (4) Road Development and Improvement.

7. Identify current and projected Refuge equipment and storage facility needs.

8. Establish a habitat classification system for documenting the current habitat types of the Refuge and to monitor changes.

Ongoing

1. Ensure natural waterflow patterns through the Refuge are not adversely affected by human or animal (beaver) activity. Locate beaver ponds and remove dams as needed to prevent damage from permanent flooding.

2. Identify habitat used by listed and candidate species. As needed, protect habitats that harbor species of special significance through closing public access

3. Monitor water quality of all waters on the Refuge.

4.   Provide protection for bald eagles, and inform the public regarding status and presence on the Refuge.

5.   Research habitat needs of listed and candidate species that might be found on the Refuge and determine if suitable habitat may be found on the Refuge. Conduct surveys to locate specimens and compile location and population data.

6.   Protect bird roosting and feeding areas from disturbance.

7.   Control and remove livestock that stray onto the Refuge.

8.   Protect trees containing cavities that may be used by wood ducks for nesting.

9.   Manage waterfowl hunting to sustain healthy populations. Protect nesting and wintering waterfowl from illegal disturbance.

10.   Monitor population levels of migratory birds to determine the success of management techniques.

11.   Protect the deer, waterfowl, and other wildlife species from illegal activity through frequent patrols.

12.   Install Refuge boundary fencing in a manner that prevents entanglement by deer as additional lands are acquired.

13.   Monitor rabbit and squirrel populations to determine status.

14.   Ensure that potential impacts on cultural resources are considered for all management activities.

15.   Encourage research activities on the Refuge that will provide resource data.

16.   Provide squirrel, rabbit, deer, turkey, duck, and raccoon hunting opportunities on the Refuge.

17.   Monitor hunter and other public use to evaluate need for additional access.

18.   Establish, maintain, and enhance a biological database management system.

19.   Monitor habitat changes occurring on the Refuge.

Fiscal Year 2000

1. Evaluate the most cost effective, environmentally beneficial method for removing pine plantations and restoring native bottomland hardwood species.

2. Convert 20 acres to green tree reservoirs, designing them in a way that will benefit a variety of species in addition to waterfowl.

3. Install 50 wood duck nesting boxes.

4. Prepare a road development and improvement plan for the Refuge, pending availability of funds.

5. Map wildlife habitat use areas on the Refuge.

6. Improve existing boat launch facilities to control erosion.

7. Hire an outdoor recreation planner.

8. Prepare management plans for Habitat Management and Public Use.

9. Collect wildlife and plant species data and establish transects to monitor habitat and wildlife use changes.

Fiscal Year 2001

1. Initiate removal of pine plantations under contract.

2. Evaluate the Refuge water monitoring program and modify as needed.

3. Establish a map record of vegetational changes based on permanent transects and aerial photograph analyses.

4. Design and construct a circular auto-tour road through Unit 2.

5. Construct bank fishing access points to expand fishing opportunities to a greater number of visitors.

6. Provide universal access for fishing.

7. Prepare management plans for: Wildlife Inventory, Law Enforcement, and Disease Prevention and Control.

8. Construct a parking area in Unit 2 to accommodate 12 cars.

9. Construct a parking area in Unit 1 to accommodate 6 cars.

10. Provide interpretive signs along the tour road and at wildlife viewing stops.

11. Develop walking trails for wildlife viewing.

12. Construct an experimental 100 acre moist impoundment in Unit 2.

13. Improve boating access in Unit 2 for non-fishing public use as well as fishing public use.

14. Schedule for design and construction of a permanent Refuge headquarters and visitor contact station on Refuge lands.

Appendices

Appendix A: Little River
National Wildlife Refuge
Unit Maps

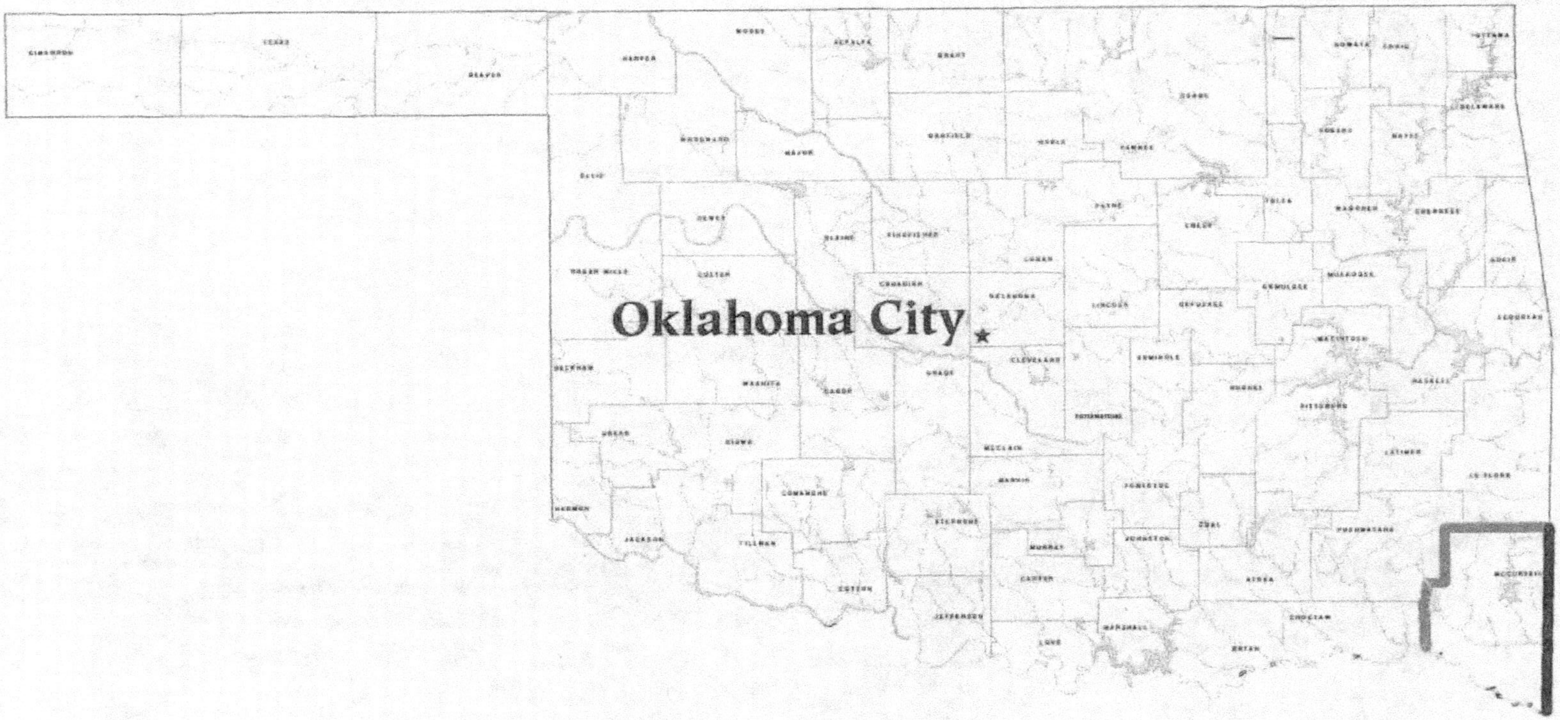

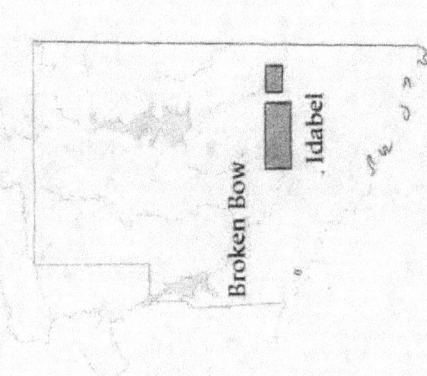

Oklahoma City ★

Broken Bow

Idabel

McCurtain County, Oklahoma

Little River National Wildlife Refuge

LITTLE RIVER NATIONAL WILDLIFE REFUGE

McCURTAIN COUNTY, OKLAHOMA

UNITED STATES
DEPARTMENT OF THE INTERIOR

UNITED STATES
FISH AND WILDLIFE SERVICE

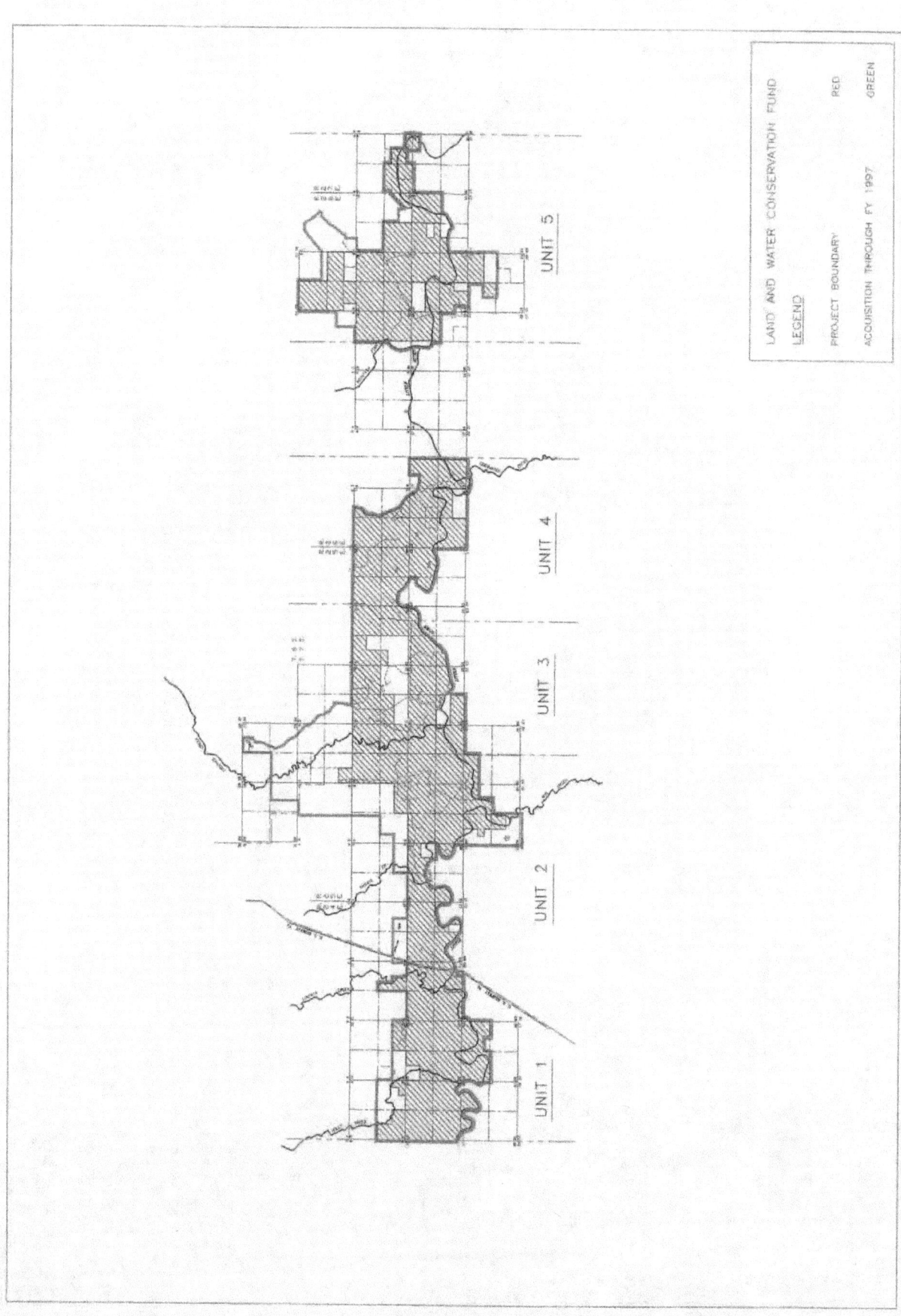

UNIT 1

UNIT 2

UNIT 3

UNIT 4

UNIT 5

INDIAN MERIDIAN

SCALE

0   3000   6000   12000   18000   FEET

LAND AND WATER CONSERVATION FUND

LEGEND

PROJECT BOUNDARY   RED

ACQUISITION THROUGH FY 1997   GREEN

COMPILED IN REALTY FRESH
DENOTED U.S.G.S. QUADRANGLE
MAPS, U.S.F.W.S. SURVEYS AND
OTHER OFFICIAL INFORMATION.

ALBUQUERQUE, NEW MEXICO   JANUARY, 1994
REVISION: 1/98

LITTLE RIVER NATIONAL WILDLIFE REFUGE
McCURTAIN COUNTY, OKLAHOMA

UNITED STATES
DEPARTMENT OF THE INTERIOR

UNITED STATES
FISH AND WILDLIFE SERVICE

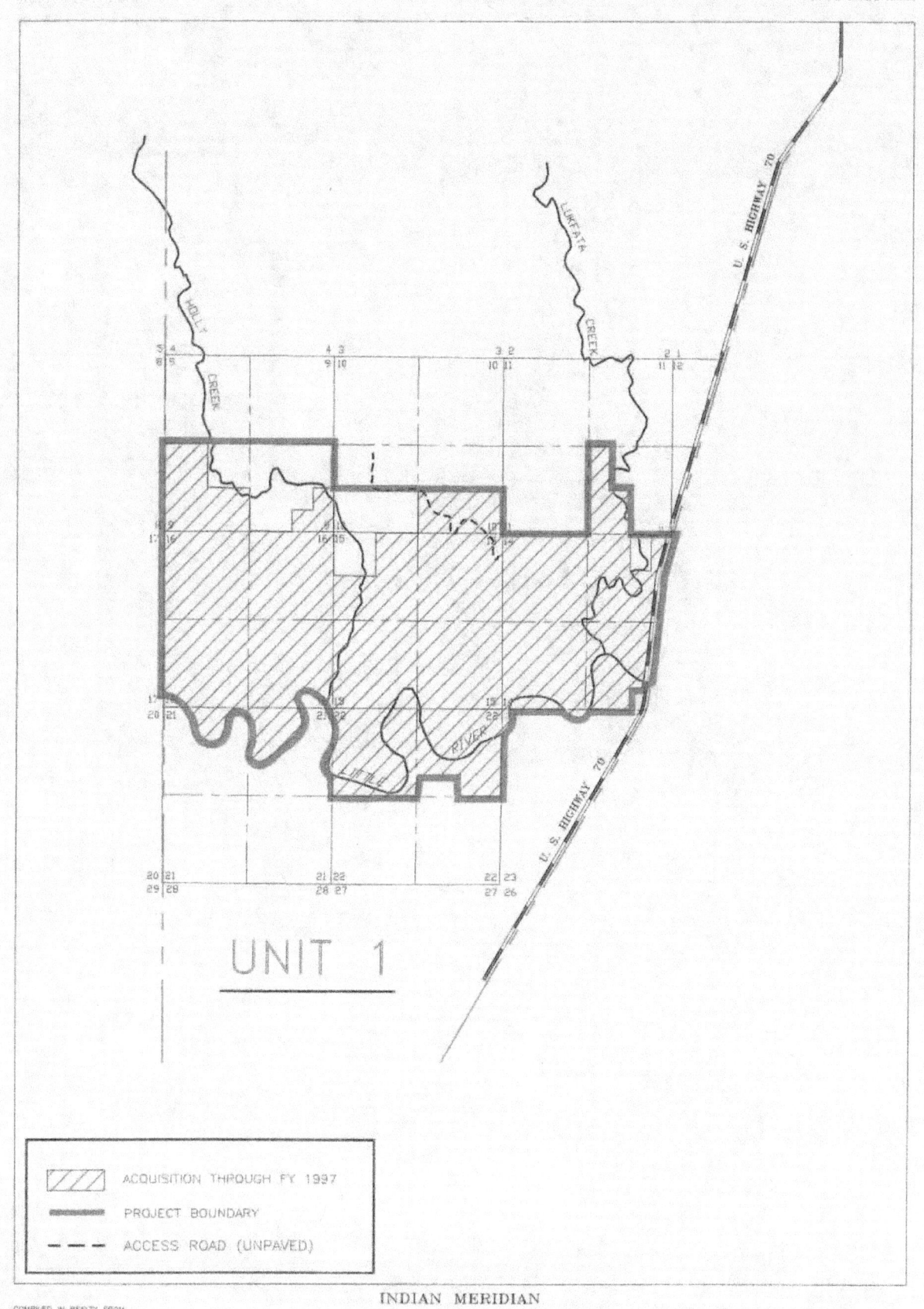

UNIT 1

ACQUISITION THROUGH FY 1997

PROJECT BOUNDARY

ACCESS ROAD (UNPAVED)

INDIAN MERIDIAN

COMPILED IN REALTY FROM
DIGITIZED U.S.G.S. QUADRANGLE
MAPS, U.S.F.W.S. SURVEYS AND
OTHER OFFICIAL INFORMATION.

ALBUQUERQUE, NEW MEXICO   SEPTEMBER, 1998

SCALE   0   2000   4000   6000   8000 FEET

SCALE   0   1   2   KILOMETERS

MEAN
DECLINATION
1975

2R OKLA SPCL

LITTLE RIVER NATIONAL WILDLIFE REFUGE
McCURTAIN COUNTY, OKLAHOMA

UNITED STATES
DEPARTMENT OF THE INTERIOR

UNITED STATES
FISH AND WILDLIFE SERVICE

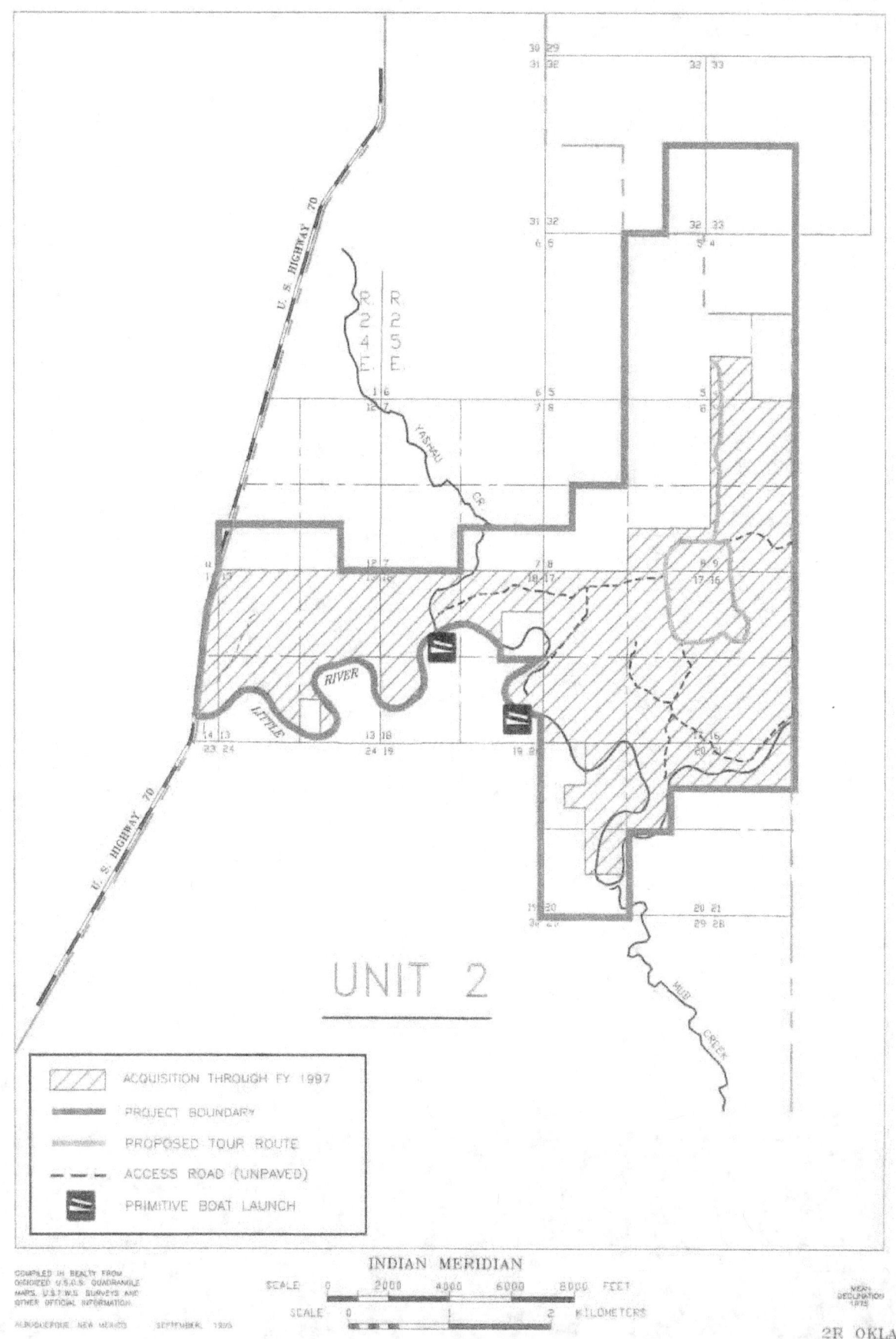

UNIT 2

ACQUISITION THROUGH FY 1997

PROJECT BOUNDARY

PROPOSED TOUR ROUTE

ACCESS ROAD (UNPAVED)

PRIMITIVE BOAT LAUNCH

INDIAN MERIDIAN

COMPILED IN REALTY FROM
DIGITIZED U.S.G.S. QUADRANGLE
MAPS, U.S.F.W.S. SURVEYS AND
OTHER OFFICIAL INFORMATION.

ALBUQUERQUE, NEW MEXICO   SEPTEMBER, 1995

SCALE   0   2000   4000   6000   8000 FEET

SCALE   0   1   2   KILOMETERS

MEAN
DECLINATION
1975

2R OKLA.

LITTLE RIVER NATIONAL WILDLIFE REFUGE

McCURTAIN COUNTY, OKLAHOMA

UNITED STATES
DEPARTMENT OF THE INTERIOR

UNITED STATES
FISH AND WILDLIFE SERVICE

T. 6 S.
T. 7 S.

UNIT 3

/////	ACQUISITION THROUGH FY 1997
	PROJECT BOUNDARY
— — —	ACCESS ROAD (UNPAVED)
	PRIMITIVE BOAT LAUNCH

INDIAN MERIDIAN

SCALE 0   2000   4000   6000   8000 FEET

SCALE 0   1   2 KILOMETERS

COMPILED IN REALTY FROM
DIGITIZED U.S.G.S. QUADRANGLE
MAPS, U.S.F.W.S. SURVEYS AND
OTHER OFFICIAL INFORMATION.

ALBUQUERQUE, NEW MEXICO   SEPTEMBER, 1998

MEAN
DECLINATION
1975

2R OKLA. SPCL

LITTLE RIVER NATIONAL WILDLIFE REFUGE

McCURTAIN COUNTY, OKLAHOMA

UNITED STATES
DEPARTMENT OF THE INTERIOR

UNITED STATES
FISH AND WILDLIFE SERVICE

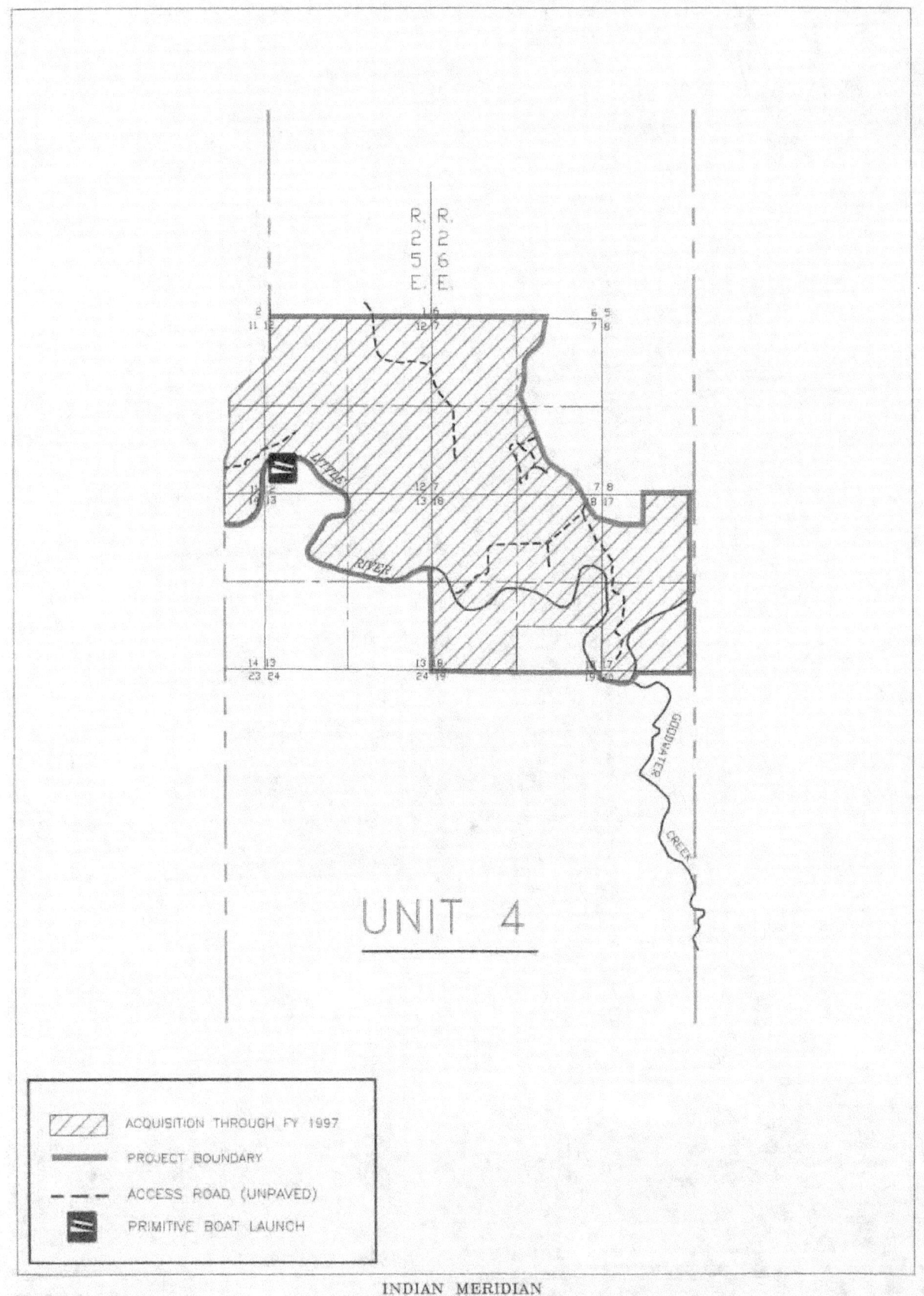

UNIT 4

ACQUISITION THROUGH FY 1997

PROJECT BOUNDARY

ACCESS ROAD (UNPAVED)

PRIMITIVE BOAT LAUNCH

INDIAN MERIDIAN

SCALE 0 2000 4000 6000 8000 FEET

SCALE 0 1 2 KILOMETERS

COMPILED IN REALTY FROM
DIGITIZED U.S.G.S. QUADRANGLE
MAPS, U.S.F.W.S. SURVEYS AND
OTHER OFFICIAL INFORMATION

ALBUQUERQUE, NEW MEXICO   SEPTEMBER 1996

MEAN
DECLINATION
1975

2R OKLA. SPCL

LITTLE RIVER NATIONAL WILDLIFE REFUGE
McCURTAIN COUNTY, OKLAHOMA

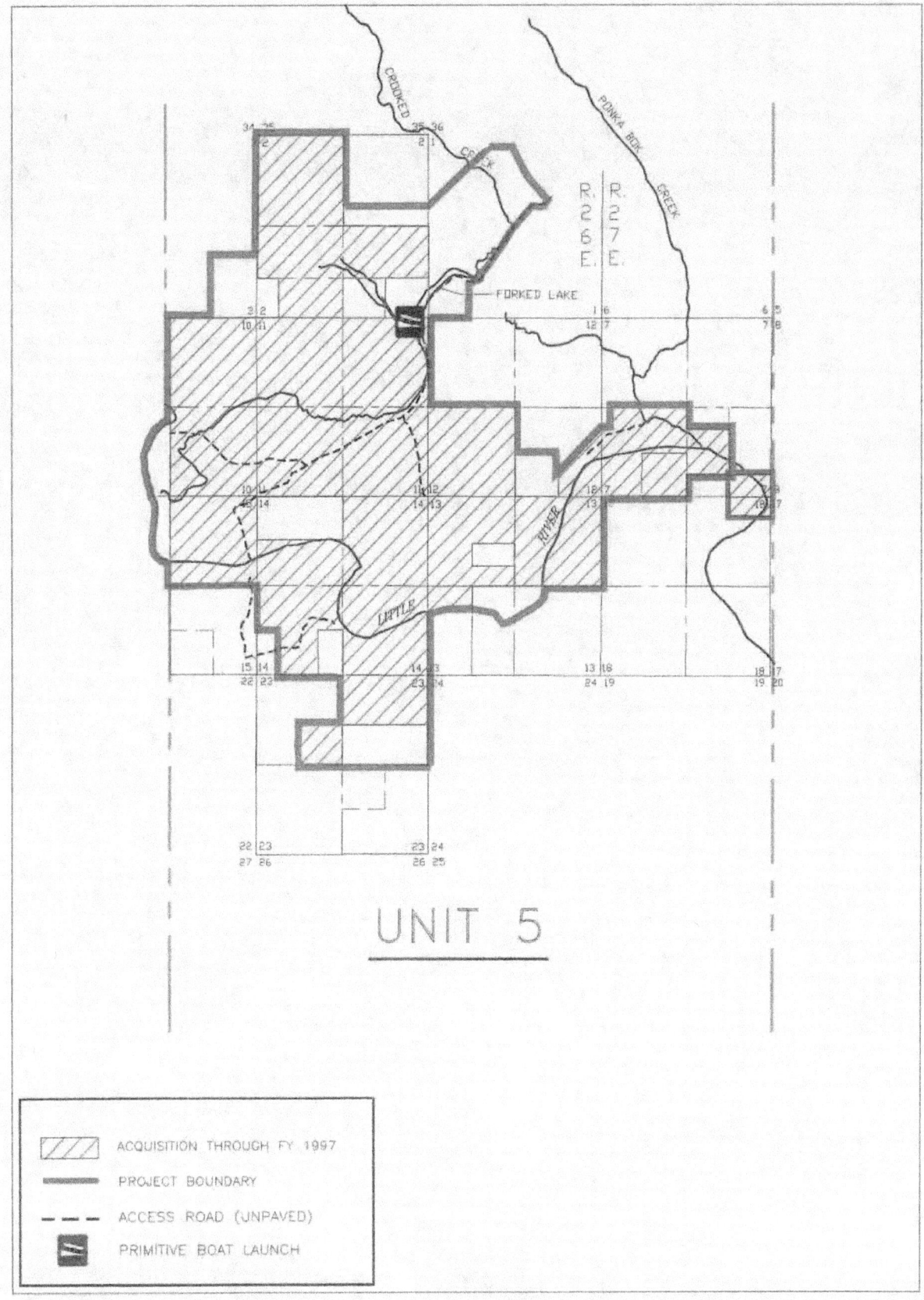

UNIT 5

////	ACQUISITION THROUGH FY 1997
▬▬▬	PROJECT BOUNDARY
– – –	ACCESS ROAD (UNPAVED)
▬	PRIMITIVE BOAT LAUNCH

INDIAN MERIDIAN

SCALE 0   2000   4000   6000   8000 FEET

SCALE 0   1   2 KILOMETERS

COMPILED IN REALTY FROM
DIGITIZED U.S.G.S. QUADRANGLE
MAPS, U.S.F.W.S. SURVEYS AND
OTHER OFFICIAL INFORMATION.

ALBUQUERQUE NEW MEXICO   SEPTEMBER, 1995

MEAN
DECLINATION
1975

2R OKLA. SPCL

Appendix B: Species that Occur, or are Likely to Occur, on Little River National Wildlife Refuge

Reptiles and Amphibians[16]

Salamanders

Western lesser siren	*Siren intermedia nettingi*
Central newt	*Notophthalmus viridescens louisianensis*
Red river mudpuppy	*Necturus maculosus louisianensis*
Three-toed amphiuma	*Amphiuma tridactylum*
Spotted salamander	*Ambystoma maculatum*
Marbled salamander	*Ambystoma opacum*
Mole salamander	*Ambystoma talpoideum*
Ouachita dusky salamander	*Desmognathus brimleyorum*
Small-mouthed salamander	*Ambystoma texanum*
Barred tiger salamander	*Ambystoma tigrinum mavortium*
Four-toed salamander	*Hemidactylium scutatum*
Western slimy salamander	*Plethodon g. glutinosus*
Southern red-backed salamander	*Plethodon serratus*

Toads

Hurters spadefoot	*Scaphiopus holbrooki hurteri*
Dwarf American toad	*Bufo americanus charlesmithi*
Woodhouse's toad	*Bufo w. woodhousei*

Frogs

Blanchard's cricket frog	*Acris crepitans blanchardi*
Bird-voiced treefrog	*Hyla avivoca*
Cope's gray treefrog	*Hyla chrysoscelis*
Green treefrog	*Hyla cinerea*
Spring peeper	*Hyla crucifer*
Eastern gray treefrog	*Hyla v. versicolor*
Eastern narrow-mouthed toad	*Pseudacris triseriata feriarum*
Upland chorus frog	*Gastrophryne carolinensis*
Bullfrog	*Rana catesbeiana*
Bronze frog	*Rana clamitans melanota*

---

[16] This information is based primarily on data furnished by Dr. Stanley Fox, Oklahoma State University, Dr. Laurie Vitt, University of Oklahoma, and Berlin Heck, Manager of Little River National Wildlife Refuge.

Pickerel frog	*Rana palustris*
Southern leopard frog	*Rana sphenocephala*

Turtles

Mississippi mud turtle	*Kinosternon subrubrum hippocrepis*
Razor-backed musk turtle	*Sternotherus carinatus*
Common musk turtle	*Sternotherus odoratus*
Snapping turtle	*Chelydra serpentina*
Aligator snapping turtle	*Macroclemys temminckii*
Southern painted turtle	*Chrysemys picta dorsalis*
Chicken turtle	*Deirochelys reticularia*
Mississippi map turtle	*Graptemys kohnii*
Ouachita map turtle	*Graptemys ouachitensis*
Eastern river cooter	*Pseudemys c. concinna*
Missouri cooter	*Pseudemys floridana hoyi*
Red-eared turtle	*Trachemys scripta elegans*
Three-toed box turtle	*Terrepene carolina triunguis*
Midland smooth softshell	*Apalone m. muticus*
Pallid spiny softshell	*Apalone spiniferus pallidus*

Lizards

Green anole	*Anolis carolinensis*
Eastern fence lizard	*Sceloporus undulatus hyacinthinus*
Six-lined racerunner	*Cnemidophorus s. sexlineatus*
Southern coal skink	*Eumeces anthracinus pluvialis*
Five-lined skink	*Eumeces fasciatus*
Broad-headed skink	*Eumeces laticeps*
Ground skink	*Scincella lateralis*
Western slender glass lizard	*Ophisaurus a. attenuatus*

Snakes

Western worm snake	*Carphophis amoenus vermis*
Mississippi ring-necked snake	*Diadophis punctatus strictogenys*
Black rat snake	*Elaphe o. obsoleta*
Western mud snake	*Farancia abacura reinwardti*
Eastern hog-nosed snake	*Heterodon platyrhinos*
Speckled kingsnake	*Lampropeltis getulus holbrooki*
Louisiana milk snake	*Lampropeltis triangulum amaura*
Eastern coachwhip	*Masticophis f. flagellum*
Yellow-bellied water snake	*Nerodia erythrogaster flavigaster*
Broad-banded water snake	*Nerodia fasciata confluens*
Diamond-backed water snake	*Nerodia r. rhombifera*
Midland water snake	*Nerodia pedon pleuralis*

Rough green snake	*Opheodrys aestivus*
Graham's crayfish snake	*Regina grahamii*
Gulf crayfish snake	*Regina rigida sinicola*
Texas brown snake	*Storeria dekayi texana*
Midland brown snake	*Storeria dekayi wrightorium*
Northern red-bellied snake	*Storeria o. occipitomaculata*
Flat-headed snake	*Tantilla gracilis*
Western ribbon snake	*Thamnophis p. proximus*
Red-sided garter snake	*Thamnophis sirtalis parietalis*
Central-lined snake	*Tripidoclonion lineatum annectens*
Western earth snake	*Virginia valeriae elegans*
Southern copperhead	*Agkistrodon c. contortrix*
Western cottonmouth	*Agkistrodon piscivorus leucostoma*
Canebrake rattlesnake	*Crotalus horridus atricaudatus*
Western pigmy rattlesnake	*Sistrurus miliarius streckeri*

Crocodilians

American alligator	*Alligator mississippiensis*

Birds[17]

Grebes

Pied-billed grebe	*Podilymbus podiceps*

Pelicans

American white pelican	*Pelecanus erythrorhynchos*

Cormorants

Double-crested cormorant	*Phalocrocorax auritus*

Anhingas

Anhinga	*Anhinga anhinga*

Bitterns, Herons, and Egrets

American bittern	*Botaurus lentiginosus*
Least bittern	*Ixobrychus exilis*
Great blue heron	*Ardea herodias*
Great egret	*Ardea alba*

---

[17] This list is based primarily on data furnished by Dr. Bill Carter, Ada, Oklahoma. An * indicates neotropical migratory land bird.

Snowy egret	*Egretta thula*
Little blue heron	*Egretta caerulea*
Cattle egret	*Bubulcus ibis*
Green heron	*Butorides striatus*
Yellow-crowned night-heron	*Nyctanassa violaceaus*

Ibises
White-faced ibis	*Plegadis chihi*

Ducks, Geese, and Swans
Greater white-fronted goose	*Anser albifrons*
Snow goose	*Chen caerulescens*
Canada goose	*Branta canadensis*
Wood duck	*Aix sponsa*
Green-winged teal	*Anas crecca*
Mallard	*Anas platyrhynchos*
American black duck	*Anas rubripes*
Northern pintail	*Anas acuta*
Blue-winged teal	*Anas discors*
Northern shoveler	*Anas clypeata*
Gadwall	*Anas strepera*
American wigeon	*Anas americana*
Ring-necked duck	*Aythya collaris*
Lesser scaup	*Aythya affinis*
Common goldeneye	*Bucephala clangula*
Bufflehead	*Bucephala albeaola*
Hooded merganser	*Lophodytes cucullatus*
Ruddy duck	*Oxyura jamaicensis*

American Vultures
Black vulture	*Coragyps atratus*
Turkey vulture*	*Cathartes aura*

Kites, Eagles, and Hawks
Osprey*	*Pandion haliaetus*
Mississippi kite*	*Ictinia mississippiensi*
Bald eagle*	*Haliaetus leucocephaluss*
Northern harrier*	*Circus cyaneus*
Sharp-shinned hawk*	*Accipiter striatus*
Cooper's hawk*	*Accipiter cooperii*
Red-shouldered hawk*	*Buteo lineatus*
Broad-winged hawk*	*Buteo platypterus*
Swainson's hawk*	*Buteo swainsoni*
Red-tailed hawk*	*Buteo jamaicensis*

Golden eagle*   *Aquila chrysaetos*

Falcons
American kestrel*   *Falco sparverius*
Merlin*   *Falco columbarius*

Turkey and Quail
Wild turkey   *Meleagris gallopavo*
Northern bobwhite   *Colinus virginianus*

Rails
Virginia rail   *Rallus limicola*
Sora   *Porzana carolina*
Common moorhen   *Gallinula chloropus*
American coot   *Fulica americana*

Plovers
Killdeer*   *Charadrius vociferus*

Sandpipers
Greater yellowlegs   *Tringa melanoleuca*
Lesser yellowlegs   *Tringa flavipes*
Solitary sandpiper   *Tringa solitaria*
Spotted sandpiper   *Actitis macularia*
Least sandpiper   *Calidris minutilla*
Long-billed dowitcher   *Limnodromus scolopaceus*
American woodcock   *Scolopax minor*

Gulls and Terns
Ring-billed gull   *Larus delawarensis*
Franklin's gull   *Larus pipixcan*

Pigeons and Doves
Mourning dove*   *Zenaida macroura*

Cuckoos and Roadrunners
Black-billed cuckoo*   *Coccyzus erythrophthalmus*
Yellow-billed cuckoo*   *Coccyzus americanus*
Greater roadrunner   *Geococcyx californianus*

Typical Owls
Eastern screech-owl   *Otus asio*
Great horned owl   *Bubo virginianus*
Barred owl   *Strix varia*

Goatsuckers
Common nighthawk*   *Chordeiles minor*
Chuck-will's-widow*   *Caprimulgus carolinensis*
Whip-poor-will*   *Caprimulgus vociferus*

Swifts
Chimney swift*   *Chaetura pelagica*

Hummingbirds
Ruby-throated hummingbird* *Archilochus colubris*

Kingfishers
Belted kingfisher*   *Ceryle alcyon*

Woodpeckers
Red-headed woodpecker   *Melanerpes erythrocephalus*
Red-bellied woodpecker   *Melanerpes carolinus*
Yellow-bellied sapsucker* *Sphyrapicus varius*
Downy woodpecker   *Picoides villosus*
Northern flicker*   *Colaptes auratus*
Pileated woodpecker   *Dryocopus pileatus*

Tyrant Flycatchers
Olive-sided flycatcher*   *Contopus borealis*
Eastern wood-pewee*   *Contopus virens*
Acadian flycatcher*   *Empidonax virescens*
Least flycatcher*   *Empidonax minimus*
Eastern phoebe*   *Sayornis phoebe*
Great crested flycatcher* *Myiarchus crinitus*
Eastern kingbird*   *Tyrannus tyrannus*
Scissor-tailed flycatcher* *Tyrannus forficatus*

Larks
Horned lark*   *Eremophila alpestris*

Swallows
Purple martin*   *Progne subis*
Tree swallow*   *Tachycineta bicolor*
Northern rough-winged swallow* *Selgidopteryx serripennis*
Bank swallow*   *Riparia riparia*
Cliff swallow*   *Hirundo pyrrhonota*
Barn swallow*   *Hirundo rustica*

Jays and Crows
Blue jay   *Cyanocitta cristata*
American crow   *Corvus brachyrhynchos*
Fish crow   *Corvus ossifragus*

Chickadees and Titmice
Carolina chickadee   *Parus carolinensis*
Tufted titmouse   *Parus bicolor*

Nuthatches
Red-breasted nuthatch   *Sitta canadensis*
White-breasted nuthatch   *Sitta carolinensis*
Brown-headed nuthatch   *Sitta pusilla*

Creepers
Brown creeper*   *Certhia americana*

Wrens
Carolina wren   *Thryothorus ludivicianus*
Bewick's wren   *Thryomanes bewickii*
House wren*   *Troglodytes aedon*
Winter wren   *Troglodytes troglodytes*
Sedge wren*   *Cistothorus platensis*
Marsh wren*   *Cistothorus palustris*

Kinglets and Gnatcatchers
Golden-crowned kinglet*   *Regulus satrapa*
Ruby-crowned kinglet*   *Regulus calendula*
Blue-gray gnatcatcher*   *Polioptila caerulea*

Thrushes
Eastern bluebird*   *Sialia sialis*
Veery*   *Catharus fuscescens*
Gray-cheeked thrush   *Catharus minimus*
Swainson's thrush*   *Catharus ustulatus*
Hermit thrush*   *Catharus guttatus*
Wood thrush*   *Hylocichla mustelina*
American robin*   *Turdus migratorius*

Mockingbirds and Thrashers
Gray catbird*   *Dumetella carolinensis*
Northern mockingbird*   *Mimus polyglottos*
Brown thrasher   *Toxostoma rufum*

Pipits
American pipit*   *Anthus rubescens*

Waxwings
Cedar waxwing*   *Bombycilla cedrorum*

Shrikes
Loggerhead shrike*   *Lanius ludovicianus*

Starlings
European starling*   *Sturnus vulgaris*

Vireos
White-eyed vireo*   *Vireo griseus*
Bell's vireo*   *Vireo bellii*
Solitary vireo*   *Vireo solitarius*
Yellow-throated vireo*   *Vireo flavifrons*
Warbling vireo*   *Vireo gilvus*
Philadelphia vireo*   *Vireo philadelphicus*
Red-eyed vireo*   *Vireo olivaceus*

Wood-Warblers
Blue-winged warbler*   *Vermivora pinus*
Golden-winged warbler*   *Vermivora chrysoptera*
Tennessee warbler*   *Vermivora peregrina*
Orange-crowned warbler   *Vermivora celata*
Nashville warbler*   *Vermivora ruficapilla*
Northern parula*   *Parula americana*
Yellow warbler*   *Dendroica petechia*
Chestnut-sided warbler*   *Dendroica pensylvanica*
Magnolia warbler*   *Dendroica magnolia*
Yellow-rumped warbler*   *Dendroica coronata*
Black-throated green warbler*   *Dendroica virens*
Blackburnian warbler*   *Dendroica fusca*
Yellow-throated warbler*   *Dendroica dominica*
Pine warbler   *Dendroica pinus*
Prairie warbler*   *Dendroica discolor*
Blackpoll warbler*   *Dendroica striata*
Cerulean warbler*   *Dendroica cerulea*
Black-and-white warbler*   *Minotilta varia*
American redstart*   *Setophaga ruticilla*
Prothonotary warbler*   *Protonotaria citrea*
Worm-eating warbler*   *Helmitheros vermivorus*
Swainson's warbler*   *Limnothlypis swainsonii*

Ovenbird*	*Seiurus aurocapillus*
Northern waterthrush*	*Seiurus noveboracensis*
Louisiana waterthrush*	*Seiurus motacilla*
Kentucky warbler*	*Oporornis formosus*
Mourning warbler*	*Oporornis philadelphia*
Common yellowthroat*	*Geothlypis trichas*
Hooded warbler*	*Wilsonia citrina*
Wilson's warbler*	*Wilsonia pusilla*
Yellow-breasted chat*	*Icteria virens*

Tanagers

Summer tanager*	*Piranga rubra*
Scarlet tanager*	*Piranga olivacea*

Cardinals, Grosbeaks, and Buntings

Northern cardinal	*Cardinalis cardinalis*
Rose-breasted grosbeak*	*Pheucticus ludovicianus*
Blue grosbeak*	*Guiraca caerulea*
Indigo bunting*	*Passerina cyanea*
Painted bunting*	*Passerina ciris*
Dickcissel*	*Spiza americana*

Sparrows, Towhees, and Allies

Eastern towhee*	*Pipilo erythrophthalmus*
Spotted towhee*	*Pipilo maculatus*
Bachman's sparrow	*Aimophila aestivalis*
Chipping sparrow*	*Spizella passerina*
Field sparrow	*Spizella pusilla*
Vesper sparrow*	*Pooecetes gramineus*
Lark sparrow*	*Chondestes grammacus*
Savannah sparrow*	*Passerculus sandwichensis*
Grasshopper sparrow*	*Ammodramus savannarum*
LeConte's sparrow	*Ammodramus leconteii*
Fox sparrow*	*Passerella iliaca*
Song sparrow*	*Melospiza melodia*
Lincoln's sparrow*	*Melospiza lincolnii*
Swamp sparrow*	*Melospiza georgiana*
White-throated sparrow*	*Zonotrichia albicollis*
White-crowned sparrow*	*Zonotrichia leucophrys*
Harris' sparrow	*Zonotrichia querula*
Dark-eyed junco*	*Junco hyemalis*

Blackbirds and Orioles

Red-winged blackbird*	*Agelaius phoeniceus*

Eastern meadowlark*	Sturnella magna
Rusty blackbird	Euphagus carolinus
Great-tailed grackle	Quiscalus mexicanus
Common grackle	Quiscalus quiscula
Brown-headed cowbird*	Molothrus ater
Orchard oriole*	Icterus spurius
Baltimore oriole*	Icterus galbula

Finches

Purple finch*	Carpodacus purpureus
Pine siskin*	Carduelis pinus
American goldfinch*	Carduelis tristis

Fish

Petromyzonidae (Lampreys)

| Chestnut lamprey | Ichthyomyzon castaneus |
| Southern brook lamprey | Ichthyomyzon gagei |

Polyodontidae (Paddlefish)

| Paddlefish | Polyodon spathula |

Leplsosteidae (Gars)

Spotted gar	Lepisosteus oculatus
Longnose gar	Lepisosteus osseus
Shortnose gar	Lepisosteus platostomus
Alligator gar	Lepisosteus spatula

Amidae (Bowfin)

| Bowfin | Amia calva |

Clupeidae (Herrings)

| Skipjack herring | Alosa chrysochloris |
| Gizzard shad | Dorosoma cepedianum |

Hiodontidae (Mooneyes)

| Goldeye | Hiodon alosoides |

Salmonidae (Trouts)

| Rainbow trout | Oncorhynchus mykiss |
| Brown trout | Salmo trutta |

Esocidae (Pikes)
Grass pickerel — *Esox americanus*

Cyprinidae (Minnows)
Grass carp — *Ctenopharyngodon idella*
Red shiner — *Cyprinella lutrensis*
Blacktail shiner — *Cyprinella venusta*
Steelcolor shiner — *Cyprinella whipplei*
Common carp — *Cyprinus carpio*
Cypress minnow — *Hybognathus hayi*
Mississippi silvery minnow — *Hybognathus nuchalis*
Plains minnow — *Hybognathus placitus*
Common shiner — *Luxilus cornutus*
Ribbon shiner — *Lythrurus fumes*
Ouachita shiner — *Lythrurus snelsoni*
Redfin shiner — *Lythrurus umbratilis*
Golden shiner — *Notemigonus crysoleucas*
Pallid shiner — *Notropis amnis*
Emerald shiner — *Notropis atherinoides*
Blackspot shiner — *Notropis atrocaudalis*
Bigeye shiner — *Notropis boops*
Ghost shiner — *Notropis buchanani*
Ironcolor shiner — *Notropis chalybaeus*
Bluehead shiner — *Notropis hubbsi*
Taillight shiner — *Notropis maculatus*
Peppered shiner — *Notropis perpallidus*
Rosyface shiner — *Notropis rubellus*
Rocky shiner — *Notropis suttkusi*
Mimic shiner — *Notropis volucellus*
Pugnose shiner — *Opsopoeodus emiliae*
Suckermouth shiner — *Phenacobius mirabilis*
Bluntnose minnow — *Pimephales notatus*
Bullhead minnow — *Pimephales vigilax*
Creek chub — *Semotilus atromaculatus*

Catostomidae (Suckers)
River carpsucker — *Carpiodes carpio*
Creek chubsucker — *Erimyzon oblongus*
Lake chubsucker — *Erimyzon sucetta*
Smallmouth buffalo — *Ictiobus bubalus*
Largemouth buffalo — *Ictiobus cyprinellus*
Black buffalo — *Ictiobus niger*
Spotted sucker — *Minytrema melanops*
River redhorse — *Moxostoma carinatum*

Black redhorse	*Moxostoma duquesnei*
Golden redhorse	*Moxostoma erythrurum*

Ictaluridae (Bullhead Catfishes)
Black bullhead	*Ameiurus melas*
Yellow bullhead	*Ameiurus natalis*
Blue catfish	*Ictalurus furcatus*
Channel catfish	*Ictalurus punctatus*
Mountain madtom	*Noturus eleutherus*
Tadpole madtom	*Noturus gyrinus*
Freckled madtom	*Noturus nocturnus*
Flathead catfish	*Pylodictis olivaris*

Aphredoderidae (Pirate Perches)
Pirate perch	*Aphredoderus sayanus*

Cyprinodontidae (Topminnows)
Golden topminnow	*Fundulus chrysotus*
Starhead topminnow	*Fundulus dispar*
Blackstripe topminnow	*Fundulus notatus*
Blackspotted topminnow	*Fundulus olivaceus*

Poeciliidae (Livebearers)
Western mosquitofish	*Gambusia affinis*

Atherinidae (Silversides)
Brook silverside	*Labidesthes sicculus*
Inland silverside	*Menidia beryllina*

Percichthyidae (Temperate basses)
White bass	*Morone chrysops*
Yellow bass	*Morone mississippiensis*

Centrarchidae (Sunfish)
Flier	*Centrarchus macropterus*
Banded pygmy sunfish	*Elassoma zonatum*
Green sunfish	*Lepomis cyanellus*
Warmouth	*Lepomis gulosus*
Orangespotted sunfish	*Lepomis humilis*
Bluegill	*Lepomis macrochirus*
Dollar sunfish	*Lepomis marginatus*
Longear sunfish	*Lepomis megalotis*
Redear sunfish	*Lepomis microlophus*
Spotted sunfish	*Lepomis punctatus*

Bantam sunfish	*Lepomis symmetricus*
Smallmouth bass	*Micropterus dolomieui*
Spotted bass	*Micropterus punctulatus*
Largemouth bass	*Micropterus salmoides*
White crappie	*Pomoxis annularis*
Black crappie	*Pomoxis nigromaculatus*

Percidae (Perches)

Crystal darter	*Ammocrypta asprella*
Scaly sand darter	*Ammocrypta vivax*
Mud darter	*Etheostoma asprigene*
Bluntnose darter	*Etheostoma chlorosomum*
Creole darter	*Etheostoma collettei*
Swamp darter	*Etheostoma fusiforme*
Slough darter	*Etheostoma gracile*
Harlequin darter	*Etheostoma histrio*
Johnny darter	*Etheostoma nigrum*
Goldstripe darter	*Etheostoma parvipinne*
Cypress darter	*Etheostoma proeliare*
Orangebelly darter	*Etheostoma radiosum*
Orangethroat darter	*Etheostoma spectabile*
Logperch	*Percina caprodes*
Channel darter	*Percina copelandi*
Bigscale logperch	*Percina macrolepida*
Blackside darter	*Percina maculata*
Slenderhead darter	*Percina phoxocephala*
Dusky darter	*Percina sciera*
River darter	*Percina shumardi*

Sciaenidae (Drums)

Freshwater drum	*Aplodinotus grunniens*

Mammals

Cottontail rabbit	*Sylvilagus floridanus*
Swamp rabbit	*Sylvilagus aquaticus*
White-tailed deer	*Odocoileus virginianus*
Beaver	*Castor canadensis*
Coyote	*Canis latrans*
Grey fox	*Urocyon cinereoargenteus*
Red fox	*Vulpes vulpes*
Virginia opossum	*Didelphis virginiana*
Nine-banded armadillo	*Dasypus novemcinctus*

Domestic pig	*Sus scrofa*
Bobcat	*Lynx rufus*
Muskrat	*Ondatra zibethicus*
Raccoon	*Procyon lotor*
River otter	*Lutra canadensis*
Striped skunk	*Mephitis mephitis*
Spotted skunk	*Spilogale putorius*
Long-tailed weasel	*Mustela frenata*
Mink	*Mustela vison*
Southern flying squirrel	*Glaucomys volans*
Grey squirrel	*Sciurus carolinensis*
Fox squirrel	*Sciurus niger*
Plains pocket gopher	*Geomys bursarius*
Eastern woodrat	*Neotoma floridana*
Golden mouse	*Ochrotomys nuttalli*
Marsh rice rat	*Oryzomys palustris*
Cotton mouse	*Peromyscus gossypinus*
White-footed mouse	*Peromyscus leucopus*
Fulvous harvest mouse	*Reithrodontomys fulvescens*
Eastern harvest mouse	*Reithrodontomys humilis*
Hispid cotton rat	*Sigmodon hispidus*
Woodland vole	*Microtus pinetorum*
House mouse	*Mus musculus*
Norway rat	*Rattus norvegicus*
Black rat	*Rattus rattus*
Nutria	*Myocastor coypus*
Short-tailed shrew	*Blarina brevicauda*
Least shrew	*Cryptotis parva*
Eastern mole	*Scalopus aquaticus*
Big brown bat	*Eptesicus fuscus*
Silver-haired bat	*Lasionycteris noctivagans*
Red bat	*Lasiurus borealis*
Seminole bat	*Lasiurus seminolus*
Southeastern myotis bat	*Myotis austroriparius*
Keen's myotis bat	*Myotis keenii*
Little brown myotis bat	*Myotis lucifugus*
Indiana myotis bat	*Myotis sodalis*
Evening bat	*Nycticeius humeralis*
Big-eared bat	*Lecotus rafinesquii*

Trees and Shrubs

Shortleaf pine	*Pinus echinata*
Loblolly pine	*Pinus taeda*
Baldcypress	*Taxodium dichum*
Eastern redcedar	*Juniperus virginiana*
Black willow	*Salix nigra*
Water hickory	*Carya aquatica*
Nutmeg hickory	*Carya myristiciformis*
Shagbark hickory	*Carya ovata*
Mockernut hickory	*Carya tomentosa*
Black walnut	*Juglans nigra*
River birch	*Betula nigra*
American hornbeam	*Carpinus caroliniana*
Eastern hophornbeam	*Ostrya virginiana*
White oak	*Quercus alba*
Southern red oak	*Quercus falcata*
Cherrybark oak	*Quercus falcata pagodifolia*
Overcup oak	*Quercus lyrata*
Blackjack oak	*Quercus marilandica*
Swamp chestnut oak	*Quercus michauxii*
Deward's white oak	*Quercus sinuata*
Chinkapin oak	*Quercus muehlenbergii*
Water oak	*Quercus nigra*
Willow oak	*Quercus phellos*
Shumard oak	*Quercus shumardii*
Pin oak	*Quercus palustris*
Nuttall oak	*Quercus nuttallii*
Water elm	*Planera aquatica*
Winged elm	*Ulmus alata*
American elm	*Ulmus americana*
Cedar elm	*Ulmus crassifolia*
Slippery elm	*Ulmus rubra*
Osage orange	*Maclura pomifera*
Red mulberry	*Morus rubra*
Pawpaw	*Asimina triloba*
Sassafras	*Sassafras albidum*
Witch hazel	*Hamamelis virginiana*
Sweetgum	*Liquidambar styraciflua*
Sycamore	*Platanus occidentalis*
Barberry hawthorn	*Crataegus berberifolia*

Cockspur hawthorn	*Crataegus crus-galli*
Parsley hawthorn	*Crataegus marshallii*
Downey hawthorn	*Crataegus mollis*
Frosted hawthorn	*Crataegus pruinosa*
Littlehip hawthorn	*Crataegus spathulata*
Green hawthorn	*Crataegus viridis*
Mexican plum	*Prunus mexicana*
Black cherry	*Prunus serotina*
Mimosa-tree	*Albizia julibrissin*
Eastern redbud	*Cercis canadensis*
Honeylocust	*Gleditsia triacanthos*
Black locust	*Robinia pseudoacacia*
Hercules club	*Zanthoxylum clava-herculis*
Chinaberry	*Melia azedarach*
Shining sumac	*Rhus copallina*
Deciduous holly	*Ilex decidua*
American holly	*Ilex opaca*
Yaupon	*Ilex vomitoria*
Strawberry bush	*Euonymus americanus*
Boxelder	*Acer negundo*
Red maple	*Acer rubrum*
Silver Maple	*Acer saccharinum*
Sugar maple	*Acer saccharum*
Red buckeye	*Aesculus pavia*
Carolina basswood	*Tilia caroliniana*
Devil's walking stick	*Aralia spinosa*
Roughleaf dogwood	*Cornus drummondii*
Flowering dogwood	*Cornus florida*
Blackgum	*Nyssa sylvatica*
Tree sparkleberry	*Vaccinium arboreum*
Common persimmon	*Diospyros virginiana*
Sweetleaf	*Symplocos tinctoria*
Green ash	*Fraxinus pennsylvanica*
Button bush	*Cephalanthus occidentalis*
Spicebush	*Lindera benzoin*
Japanese privet	*Ligustrum japonicum*
Eastern baccharis	*Baccharis halimifolia*
Southern wax myrtle	*Myrica pussilla*
American beautyberry	*Callicarpa americana*

Appendix C: Legal, Policy, and Administrative Guidelines and Other Special Considerations

Administration of national wildlife refuges is governed by bills passed by the United States Congress and signed into law by the President of the United States, and by regulations promulgated by the various branches of the government. Following is a brief description of some of the most pertinent laws and statutes establishing legal parameters and policy direction for the National Wildlife Refuge System:

Acts of Congress

Section 10 of the Rivers and Harbors Act approved March 3, 1899 (20 Stat. 1151; 33 1151; 33 U.S.C. 403).

Prohibits unauthorized obstruction or alteration of any navigable water of the United States. Construction of any structure in or over any navigable water of the United States, excavation from or depositing of material in such waters, or accomplishment of any other work affecting the course, location condition, or capacity of such waters are unlawful unless the work has been recommended by the Chief of Engineers and authorized by the Secretary of the Army. Authority of the Secretary of the Army to prevent obstructions to navigation in navigable waters of the United States was extended to artificial islands and fixed structures located on the Outer Continental Shelf by Section 4 of the Outer Continental Shelf Lands Act of 1953 [67 Stat. 463; 43 U.S.C. 1333 (f.)].

Refuge Trespass Act of June 28, 1906 (18 U.S.C. 41; 43 Stat. 98, 18 U.S.C. 145).

Provided the first Federal protection for wildlife on national wildlife refuges. This Act made it unlawful to hunt, trap, capture, willfully disturb, or kill any bird or wild animal, or take or destroy the eggs of any such birds, on any lands of the United States set apart or reserved as refuges or breeding grounds for such birds or animals by any law, proclamation, or executive order, except under rules and regulations of the Secretary. The Act also protects government property on such lands.

Migratory Bird Treaty Act of 1918 (16 U.S.C. 703-711; 50 CFR Subchapter B), as amended.

Implements treaties with Great Britain (for Canada) and Mexico for protection of migratory birds whose welfare is a federal responsibility. Provides for regulations to control taking, possession, selling, transporting, and importing of migratory birds and provides penalties for violations.

Migratory Bird Conservation Act of 1929
(16 U.S.C. 715-s, 45 Stat. 1222), as amended.
Authorizes acquisition, development, and maintenance of migratory bird refuges; cooperation with other agencies in conservation; and investigations and publications on North American birds.

Migratory Bird Hunting Stamp Act of 1934
(16 U.S.C. 718-718h; 48 Stat. 51), as amended.
Requires that all waterfowl hunters, sixteen (16) years of age or older, possess a valid duck stamp. Net revenues from the sale of duck stamps are used to acquire migratory bird refuges and waterfowl production areas.

Criminal Code of Provisions of 1940, as amended (18 U.S.C. 41).
States the intent of Congress to protect all wildlife within federal sanctuaries, refuges, fish hatcheries, and breeding grounds. Provides that anyone, except in compliance with rules and regulations promulgated by authority of law, who hunts, traps, or willfully disturbs any such wildlife, or willfully injures, molests, or destroys any property of the United States on such land or water, shall be fined up to $500 or imprisoned for not more than 6 months or both.

Bald Eagle Act of 1940 (16 U.S.C. 668-668d;
54 Stat. 250; 50 CFR Subchapter), as amended.
Provides for protection of the bald eagle (the national emblem) and the golden eagle.

Fish and Wildlife Act of 1956 (70 Stat. 1119;
16 U.S.C. 742a-742J), as amended.
Approved August 8, 1956, this Act establishes a comprehensive fish and wildlife policy and directs the Secretary to provide continuing research; extension and information service; and directed development, management, and conservation of fish and wildlife resources.

Fish and Wildlife Recreation Act of 1972
(Public Law 87-114; 76 Stat. 653-654; 16 U.S.C.).
Authorizes appropriate, incidental, or secondary recreational use on conservation areas administered by the Secretary of the Interior for fish and wildlife purposes.

Wilderness Preservation and Management
(50 CFR 35; 78 Stat. 890; 16 U.S.C. 1131-1136; 43 U.S.C. 1201).
Provides procedures for establishing wilderness units under the Wilderness Act of 1964 on units of the National Wildlife Refuge System.

National Historic Preservation Act of 1966
(16 U.S.C. 470- 470b, 470c-470n, 80 Stat. 915), as amended.
Provides for preservation of significant historical features (buildings, objects, etc.) through a grant-in-aid program to the states. Establishes a National Register of Historic Places. Federal agencies are required to take into account effects of their actions on buildings, etc., included or eligible for inclusion on the National Register.

National Wildlife Refuge System Administration Act of 1966 (Public Law 89-669; 80 Stat. 929; 16 U.S.C. 668dd-668ee), as amended.
Authorizes the Secretary of the Interior to "permit the use of any area within the System for any purpose including, but not limited to, hunting, fishing, public recreation and accommodations, and access whenever he determines that such uses are compatible with the major purposes for which such areas were established." Consolidates authorities for the various categories of areas previously established that are administered by the Secretary of the Interior for conservation of fish and wildlife, including species that are threatened with extinction, all lands, waters, and interests therein administered by the Secretary as wildlife refuges, etc., which are hereby designated as the National Wildlife Refuge System. Provides that the Secretary may authorize hunting and fishing to the extent practicable and consistent with state fish and wildlife laws and regulations.

The National Environmental Policy Act of 1969
(42 U.S.C. 4321-4347).
Declares national policy to encourage a productive and enjoyable harmony between humans and their environment. Section 102 of that Act directs that "to the fullest extent possible: (1) the policies, regulations, and public laws of the United States shall be interpreted and administered in accordance with the policies set forth in this Act, and (2) all agencies of the Federal Government shall . . . insure that presently unquantified environmental amenities and values may be given appropriate consideration in decision making along with economic and technical considerations. . . ."

Section 102(2)c of NEPA requires all federal agencies, with respect to major federal actions significantly affecting the quality of the human environment, to submit to the Council on Environmental Quality a detailed statement on:

(i)   The environmental impact of the proposed action;
(ii)   Any adverse environmental effect which cannot be avoided should the proposal be implemented;
(iii)   Alternatives to the proposed action;
(iv)   The relationship between local short-term uses of the environment and the maintenance and enhancement of long-term productivity
(v)   Any irreversible and irretrievable commitments of resources which would be involved in the proposed action, should it be implemented.

Section 401 of the Federal Water Pollution Control Act of 1972 (Public Law 92-500; 86 Stat. 816, 33 U.S.C. 1411).

Requires any applicant for a federal license or permit to conduct any activity that may result in a discharge into navigable waters to obtain a certification from the state in which the discharge originates or will originate, or, if appropriate, from the interstate water pollution control agency having jurisdiction over navigable waters at the point where the discharge originates or will originate, that the discharge will comply with applicable effluent limitations and water quality standards. A certification obtained for construction of any facility must also pertain to subsequent operation of the facility.

Section 404 of the Federal Water Pollution Control Act of 1972 (Public Law 92-500, 86 Stat. 816).

Authorizes the Secretary of the Army, acting through the Chief of Engineers, to issue permits, after notice and opportunity for public hearings, for discharge of dredged or fill material into navigable waters at specified disposal sites. Selection of disposal sites will be in accordance with guidelines developed by the Administrator of the Environmental Protection Agency in conjunction with the Secretary of the Army. Furthermore, the Administrator can prohibit or restrict use of any defined area as a disposal site whenever she/he determines, after notice and opportunity for public hearings, that discharge of such materials into such areas will have an unacceptable adverse effect on municipal water supplies, shellfish beds, fishery areas, wildlife, or recreational areas.

Endangered Species Act of 1973 and recent amendments

(16 U.S.C. 1531-1543; 87 Stat. 884), as amended.

Provides for conservation of threatened and endangered species of fish, wildlife, and plants by federal action and by encouraging state programs. Specific provisions include: (1) the listing and determination of critical habitat of endangered and threatened species and consultation with the Service on any federally funded or licensed project that could affect any of these agencies; (2) prohibition of unauthorized taking, possession, sale, transport, etc., of endangered species; (3) an expanded program of habitat acquisition; (4) establishment of cooperative agreements and grants-in-aid to states that establish and maintain an active, adequate program for endangered and threatened species; and (5) assessment of civil and criminal penalties for violating the Act or regulations.

Refuge Revenue Sharing Act of 1978 (Public Law 95-469, approved October 17, 1978, which amended 16 U.S.C. 715s; 50 CFR, part 34).

Changed the provisions for sharing revenues with counties in a number of ways. It makes revenue sharing applicable to all lands administered by the Service, whereas previously it was applicable only to areas in the National Wildlife Refuge System. The new law makes payments available for any governmental purpose, whereas the old law restricted the use of payments to roads and schools. For fee (acquired) lands, the new law provides a payment of 75 cents per acre, 3/4 of 1 percent of fair market value or 25 percent of net receipts, whichever is greater, whereas the old law provided a payment of 3/4 of 1 percent adjustment cost or 25 percent of net receipts, whichever was greater. The new law makes reserve (public domain) lands entitlement lands under Public Law 94- 565 (16 U.S.C. 1601-1607), and provides for a payment of 25 percent of net receipts. The new law authorizes appropriations to make up any shortfall in net receipts, to make payments in the full amount for which counties are eligible. The old law provided that if net receipts were insufficient to make full payment, payment to each county would be reduced proportionately.

The National Wildlife Refuge System Improvement Act of 1997 (Public Law 105-57, October 9, 1997).

This Act defines the mission of the National Wildlife Refuge System, which is, "to administer a national network of lands and waters for the conservation, management, and where appropriate, restoration of the fish, wildlife and plant resources and their habitats within the United States for the benefit of present and future generations of Americans."

It requires the Secretary of the Interior to ensure that the biological integrity, diversity, and environmental health of the National Wildlife Refuge System are maintained.

It defines compatible wildlife-dependent recreation as "legitimate and appropriate general public use of the [National Wildlife Refuge] System." It establishes hunting, fishing, wildlife observation and photography, and environmental education and interpretation is "priority public uses" where compatible with the mission and purpose of individual national wildlife refuges.

It retains the refuge managers' authority to use sound professional judgment in determining compatible public uses on national wildlife refuges and whether or not they will be allowed. It establishes a formal process for determining "compatible use." And it requires public involvement in decisions to allow new uses of national wildlife refuges and renew existing ones, as well as in the development of "comprehensive conservation plans" for national wildlife refuges.

Regulations

Rights-of-Way General Regulations
(50 CFR 29.21; 34 FR 19907, December 19, 1969).
Provides for procedures for filing applications. Provides terms and conditions under which rights-of-way over, above, and across lands administered by the Service may be granted.

Use of Off-Road Vehicles on Public Lands (Executive Order 11644, FR Vol. 37, No. 27, February 9, 1972).
Provides policy and procedures for regulating off-road vehicles.

National Wildlife Refuge Regulations for the Most Recent
Fiscal Year (50 CFR 25-35, 43 CFR 3103.2 and 3120.3-3).
Provides regulations for administration and management of national wildlife refuges including mineral leasing, exploration, and development.

Mission and Goals

The mission of all national wildlife refuges, as defined in the National Wildlife Refuge System Improvement Act of 1997 (Public Law 105-57, October 9, 1997), is: "To administer a national network of lands and waters for the conservation, management, and where appropriate, restoration of the fish, wildlife and plant resources and their habitats within the United States for the benefit of present and future generations of Americans."

Relationship to Other Plans

North American Waterfowl Management Plan

The North American Waterfowl Management Plan guidelines were published in May 1986. The NAWMP is a broad policy framework that describes the overall scope of requirements for management of migratory waterfowl in Canada and the United States. Implementation of the NAWMP requires that these nations establish national, provincial, territorial, state, and flyway plans which convert international objectives to operational plans. A committee known as the North American Waterfowl Management Plan Committee would be established and, among other responsibilities, would update the NAWMP in 1990 and every 5 years thereafter.

The overall goal of the continental habitat program is to maintain and manage an appropriate distribution and diversity of high quality waterfowl habitat in North America that will maintain current distributions of waterfowl populations and, under average environmental conditions, sustain an abundance of waterfowl consistent with listed goals. (In broad terms, the NAWMP is designated to ensure habitat for 62 million breeding ducks on the continent and to achieve a fall flight objective of more than 100 million ducks. Habitat also will be necessary to support more than 6 million overwintering geese.) The Refuge will contribute to this goal.

Endangered/Threatened Species Recovery Plans

There are national recovery plans for bald eagles, but no plan provides guidance applicable to the Refuge. Eagle recovery plans deal mainly with nesting habitat, whereas the Refuge provides wintering habitat.

Administrative Considerations

The Refuge consists of 12,029 acres as of January 1, 1996. Title searches note valid existing easements and right-of-ways records. Existing rights-of-way give grantees the right to travel over property owned by the Service and to maintain structures such as powerlines, underground pipelines, and roads on Service property.

Archeological/Historical Sites

Archeological and historical sites within the Refuge must be identified and protected; see page 27. The Regional Historic Preservation Officer is available for assistance and the Cultural Resource Management Handbook provides guidance.

Road Rights-of-Way

A right-of-way easement granted to the State of Oklahoma for improvement to State Highway 259/70 is in effect in Sections 13 and 14, Township 7 South, Range 24 East.

Gas Pipeline Rights-of-Way

An easement of undesignated size, granted to Lone Star Gas Company for a gas pipeline, is in effect in Section 9, Township 7 South, Range 24 East.

Water Line Easement

A 15-foot easement granted to the City of Idabel for water and sewer lines passes through Section 14, Township 7 South, Range 24 East.

Power Line Utility

A 100-foot easement granted to Western Farmers Electric Cooperative for a power line is in effect in Sections 10, 15 and 22, Township 7 South, Range 24 East.

Outstanding Mineral Reservations

All oil and mineral rights on lands purchased to date were reserved by prior owners. No exploitation is occurring at present.

Commercial Beehives

Bees are important pollinators with no known detrimental effects on aesthetics or on the environment if hives are placed out of the public view. Applications for beekeeping permits on the Refuge will be considered on a case-by-case basis.

Refuge Revenue Sharing Act of 1978

The Refuge Revenue Sharing Act affected the Refuge for the first time in 1987. The payment for Refuge lands is based on a rate of 75 cents per acre, 3/4 of 1 percent of market value or 25 percent of net receipts, whichever is greater. The payment must be at least 60 percent of the total value. Payments to date are listed below.

Table B-1. Refuge Revenue Sharing Act Payments for Little River Refuge.

Year	Acres	Amount
1987	1,995	$ 4,812
1988	5,763	20,545
1989	8,782	37,444
1990	9,747	49,798
1991	11,617	55,924
1992	12,029	53,095
1993	12,029	50,638
1994	12,029	50,144
1995	12,029	42,732
1996	12,029	47,119

Land Acquisition

The Oklahoma Legislature approved the acquisition of 15,000 total acres for the Refuge in enrolled House Joint Resolution Number 1046, signed March 31, 1986. Land acquisition began in 1987 with the purchase of 1,955 acres. By the end of 1997, the Refuge included 12,029 acres.

Contaminants

No contaminants are known to exist on the Refuge. The Little River and its tributaries provide water for several industries upstream from the Refuge including a chicken processing plant, a plywood plant, and a fiberboard mill, creating a potential for contaminants to be released into the Little River and its tributaries.

Navigation Channel

The U.S. Army Corps of Engineers is studying the feasibility of water resource development opportunities within southeastern Oklahoma. The Little River is one of several systems being considered for development as a navigation channel through the area. A joint study by Corps and the Service revealed that the navigation project and the Refuge project can both be accomplished in the 15,000-acre proposed Refuge area. The Corps and the Service wrote a joint letter to Congressman Wes Watkins (the Refuge lies entirely within the Third Congressional District) stating that the navigation and Refuge projects are compatible as planned.

Major considerations necessary to prevent or reduce negative impacts to the Refuge resulting from construction of a navigation channel using the Little River are:

- Locate locks and dams outside the immediate Refuge area.

- Adjust channel alignment within the Little River floodplain to best accommodate the Refuge and minimize impacts on the Little River.

- Install appropriate water control structures at outlets of existing oxbows or drainages and new cutoffs as needed to prevent changes harmful to Refuge objectives.

- Where loss of Refuge lands cannot be avoided, acquire replacement habitat adjacent to the Refuge. This might be accomplished by addition of cutoff land parcels to the Refuge.

- Where the existing channel is widened, leave the north bank intact where possible and widen on the south bank.

- Where channel cuts occur on Refuge lands, stabilize the banks to prevent excessive erosion.

- Place spoil materials outside Refuge lands on the south side of the channel (initial and maintenance) and retain them within levees.

- Discourage port and industrial development in the immediate Refuge area.

- Maintain minimum flows in the channel, control maximum flows, and minimize sudden fluctuations to aid in water management on the Refuge.

- Acquire lands in the Refuge vicinity without timber and other reservations except on areas that will be permanently inundated.

The Service and the Corps have worked together in cooperative planning of the Little River navigation alternatives and the Refuge. The above listed considerations were taken into account during that planning process. The Corps has determined that the most important of these items and others in large degree can be accommodated to prevent, minimize, or mitigate impacts on the Refuge.

In view of these considerations, it is the opinion of the Service that the proposed navigation project on the Little River is compatible with Refuge purposes.

Hydropower Potential

In October 1988, the Bureau of Reclamation concluded a 3-year study of hydropower potential in southeastern Oklahoma. A report was compiled entitled "Report on Kiamichi Hydropower Potential," which identified economically justified sites for single-purpose hydropower development. However, future multipurpose projects at these sites may be feasible. Sites identified that would impact Refuge operations are; the Idabel site in Section 14, Township 7 South, Range 24 East; the Goodwater site in Section 17, Township 7 South, Range 26 East; and the Ponka Bok site in Section 10, Township 7 South, Range 26 East. The Idabel and Goodwater sites are on the Little River and the Ponka Bok site is on the Mountain Fork River. These three projects would flood various portions of the Refuge resulting in destruction of the bottomland hardwood resources the Refuge was established to preserve.

Other changes in hydrology resulting from hydropower projects include changes in water temperature and dissolved oxygen resulting from water releases being made from the bottom of the reservoir. Water flow stabilization would reduce or halt seasonal flooding of the Refuge, a necessary process in maintenance of bottomland hardwoods.

Other Considerations

Animal Trespass

Traditionally, cattle were released in the bottomlands for winter foraging on switchcane (*Arundinaria*) and were removed to clearcuts during other seasons of the year. Hogs were free-roaming in the bottomlands all year. Various local families had, within roughly defined boundaries, "hog claims" on land, regardless of ownership, on which all hogs belonged to that claim. All livestock

99

were free-roaming but generally managed to some degree. For example, cattle were gathered for shots and branding or moved to new grazing areas, and hogs were gathered for ear marking and neutering.

Under refuge regulations, cattle are allowed on refuges only with a permit, and no free-roaming stock are allowed under any conditions. Cattle have been fenced out of the Little River Refuge, but hogs still reproduce in the bottomlands and are extremely wild, creating a serious control problem.

Headquarters/Visitor Center Complex

Funds were appropriated for design and construction of a headquarters/visitor center complex. Siting such a complex presented problems due to the low elevation of Refuge lands. The appropriated funds were lost to a 1995 rescission.

Drug Activities and Law Enforcement

Some areas now within the Refuge were previously used for illegally growing marijuana. Plants were found and destroyed in 1987 and 1988. The problem has been resolved through law enforcement efforts.

Appendix D: Little River
National Wildlife Refuge
Refuge Operating Needs (RONS)

HQ: Little River NWR   **CD: OK03**

Proj #: 98001   **Type:** NWR   **District:** Oklahoma

Main ecosystem: Arkansas/Red Rivers

ACTIVITY: *MONITORING & STUDIES*   *Wildlife*
        1.a. Surveys & Censuses

MEASURES: 5 wildlife surveys will be conducted
                        4 habitat surveys will be conducted
                        0 % of survey will be off-refuge

TITLE:

DESCRIPTION:

This project will collect and analyze green tree reservoir management data, endangered species/critical habitat inventories, habitat mapping, and plant community composition needed for effective management of refuge lands.

FUNDS NEEDED ($1000s):

	One-Time	Recurring Base	First Year Need
Construction Costs...................	$80		
Operations: Personnel Cost..........			
Equipment Cost..........			
Facility Cost...........			
Services/Supplies.......			
Miscellaneous Costs.....			
TOTAL Operations Cost..			

PERMANENT STAFF NEEDED (FTEs):

	Number (1/10s)	FTE Cost
Managers....................................		
Biologists.................................		
Resource Specialists.......................		
Education/Recreation Staff.................		
Law Enforcement............................		
Clerical/Administrative....................		
Maintenance/Equipment Operation...........		
TOTAL FTEs Needed.......................		

PROJECT NOTES:

EMPHASIS: CHS CRP CM OI TOT   **TYPE:** CI DM TOT   **DOI RANK:** ....

OUTCOMES:

ES	WF	OMB	HEC	IAF	SDA	RW	FAR	PED	PRC	TOT
5	30	15	40	0	0	10		0	0	100

PLANNING LINK:

☒ Station CCP approved 10/97+   ☐ FWS Recovery Plan
☐ Station CCP/equivalent pre-10/97 ☒ FWS Ecosystem Goal/Plan
☒ Station Goal/Objective   ☐ Other Major Plan
☐ Station Step-down Mgmt Plan   ☐ Legal Mandate

This project will establish a biological data base necessary for effective management of the Refuge as outlined in the CMP.

RANK - STATION: ..001..   **DISTRICT:** ....   **REGIONAL:** ....   **NATIONAL:** ....

Updated October 9, 1998

21680   Little River NWR   OK
HQ: Little River NWR   CD: OK03
Proj #: 98002   Type: NWR   District: Oklahoma
Main ecosystem: Arkansas/Red Rivers

ACTIVITY: *HABITAT MANAGEMENT*   *Habitat*
           3.e. Forest Management

MEASURES: 980 acres will be harvested
                  0 acres will be treated

TITLE:

DESCRIPTION:

Begin management of pine plantations to restore to bottomland hardwoods
and encourage bottomland hardwood regeneration. Action should
dramatically improve habitats for neotropical birds and other wildlife.

FUNDS NEEDED ($1000s):	One-Time	Recurring Base	First Year Need
Construction Costs..................	$10		
Operations: Personnel Cost..........			
Equipment Cost..........			
Facility Cost..........			
Services/Supplies.......			
Miscellaneous Costs.....			
TOTAL Operations Cost..			

PERMANENT STAFF NEEDED (FTEs):	Number (1/10s)	FTE Cost
Managers............................		
Biologists..........................		
Resource Specialists................		
Education/Recreation Staff..........		
Law Enforcement.....................		
Clerical/Administrative.............		
Maintenance/Equipment Operation.....		
TOTAL FTEs Needed.................		

PROJECT NOTES:

EMPHASIS:	CHS	CRP	CM	OI	TOT	TYPE:	CI	DM	TOT	DOI RANK: ....

OUTCOMES:	ES	WF	OMB	HEC	IAF	SDA	RW	FAR	PED	PRC	TOT
	05	5	10	60	0	0	5		5	10	100

PLANNING LINK:

☒ Station CCP approved 10/97+   ☐ FWS Recovery Plan
☐ Station CCP/equivalent pre-10/97   ☒ FWS Ecosystem Goal/Plan
☒ Station Goal/Objective   ☐ Other Major Plan
☐ Station Step-down Mgmt Plan   ☐ Legal Mandate

This project will provide habitat for many species of wetland dependent wildlife and contribute to the Refuge objectives outlined in the above document.

RANK - STATION: ..002.. **DISTRICT:** .... **REGIONAL:** .... **NATIONAL:** ....

Updated October 9, 1998

```
21680    Little River NWR                                          OK
HQ: Little River NWR                              CD: OK03
Proj #: 98003        Type: NWR        District: Oklahoma
Main ecosystem: Arkansas/Red Rivers
```

┌───┐
│   │
└───┘

ACTIVITY: *HABITAT RESTORATION*   *Habitat*
      2.a.Wetland Restoration

MEASURES: 20 refuge acres will be restored
               0 off-refuge acres will be restored

TITLE:

DESCRIPTION:

Experimental green-tree impoundments will be constructed in Unit 3 and unit 4 covering 10 acres each, using low level dikes and rainfall as a water source.

FUNDS NEEDED ($1000s):	One-Time	Recurring Base	First Year Need
Construction Costs..................	$30		
Operations: Personnel Cost.........			
Equipment Cost.........			
Facility Cost..........			
Services/Supplies.......			
Miscellaneous Costs.....			
TOTAL Operations Cost..			

PERMANENT STAFF NEEDED (FTEs):	Number (1/10s)	FTE Cost
Managers.................................		
Biologists...............................		
Resource Specialists.....................		
Education/Recreation Staff...............		
Law Enforcement..........................		
Clerical/Administrative..................		
Maintenance/Equipment Operation..........		
TOTAL FTEs Needed.....................		

PROJECT NOTES:

EMPHASIS:

CHS	CRP	CM	OI	TOT

TYPE:

CI	DM	TOT

DOI RANK: ....

OUTCOMES:

ES	WF	OMB	HEC	IAF	SDA	RW	FAR	PED	PRC	TOT
5	35	20	10	0	0	10		15	5	100

PLANNING LINK:

☒ Station CCP approved 10/97+   ☐ FWS Recovery Plan
☐ Station CCP/equivalent pre-10/97   ☒ FWS Ecosystem Goal/Plan
☒ Station Goal/Objective   ☐ Other Major Plan
☐ Station Step-down Mgmt Plan   ☐ Legal Mandate

This project will provide habitat for many species of wetland
dependent wildlife and contribute to the Refuge objectives outlined in
the above documents.

RANK - STATION: ..003.   **DISTRICT:** ....   **REGIONAL:** ....   **NATIONAL:** ....

Updated October 9, 1998

21680   Little River NWR   OK
HQ: Little River NWR   CD: OK03
Proj #: 98004   Type: NWR   District: Oklahoma
Main ecosystem: Arkansas/Red Rivers

```
.................................................................................
.                                                                               .
.                                                                               .
.................................................................................
```

ACTIVITY: *PUBLIC EDUCATION & RECREATION*   *People*
            7.a. Provide Visitor Services
MEASURES: 2,000 new visitors will be served
                   1,000 existing visitors will be served
                       0 % will support the top 6 priority public uses
                       0 % will support non-priority public uses

TITLE:

DESCRIPTION:
Acquire public right-of-ways over existing privately owned roads
accessing Refuge units 2 and 4.

Unit 2 right-of-way is 24' X 4,300' (2.4 acres).

Unit 4 requires 2 right-of-ways, each 24' X 8,000' (4.4 acres).

FUNDS NEEDED ($1000s):	One-Time	Recurring Base	First Year Need
Construction Costs....................	$50		
Operations: Personnel Cost..........			
Equipment Cost..........			
Facility Cost...........			
Services/Supplies.......			
Miscellaneous Costs.....			
TOTAL Operations Cost..			

PERMANENT STAFF NEEDED (FTEs):	Number (1/10s)	FTE Cost
Managers..		
Biologists......................................		
Resource Specialists............................		
Education/Recreation Staff......................		
Law Enforcement.................................		
Clerical/Administrative.........................		
Maintenance/Equipment Operation.................		
TOTAL FTEs Needed........................		

PROJECT NOTES:

EMPHASIS:	CHS	CRP	CM	OI	TOT		TYPE:	CI	DM	TOT		DOI RANK:

OUTCOMES:	ES	WF	OMB	HEC	IAF	SDA	RW	FAR	PED	PRC	TOT
	0	0	0	0	0	0	0	0	50	50	100

PLANNING LINK:

- ☒ Station CCP approved 10/97+
- ☐ Station CCP/equivalent pre-10/97
- ☐ Station Goal/Objective
- ☐ Station Step-down Mgmt Plan
- ☐ FWS Recovery Plan
- ☐ FWS Ecosystem Goal/Plan
- ☐ Other Major Plan
- ☐ Legal Mandate

This project will provide public access to Refuge units which presently do not have legal public access across privately owned roads.

RANK - STATION: 004 **DISTRICT:** .... **REGIONAL:** .... **NATIONAL:** ....

Updated October 9, 1998

HQ: Little River NWR

Proj #: 98005   Type: NWR   District: Oklahoma

Main ecosystem: Arkansas/Red Rivers

CD: OK03

ACTIVITY: *PUBLIC EDUCATION & RECREATION*   *People*

7.a. Provide Visitor Services

MEASURES: 1,000 new visitors will be served

2,000 existing visitors will be served

0 % will support the top 6 priority public uses

0 % will support non-priority public uses

TITLE:

DESCRIPTION:

Construct 24' X 30,000' (16.5 acres) gravel top road with interpretive displays in Unit 2.

FUNDS NEEDED ($1000s):

	One-Time	Recurring Base	First Year Need
Construction Costs...................	$3,000		
Operations: Personnel Cost..........			
Equipment Cost..........			
Facility Cost...........			
Services/Supplies.......			
Miscellaneous Costs.....			
TOTAL Operations Cost..			

PERMANENT STAFF NEEDED (FTEs):

	Number (1/10s)	FTE Cost
Managers.............................		
Biologists...........................		
Resource Specialists.................		
Education/Recreation Staff...........		
Law Enforcement......................		
Clerical/Administrative..............		
Maintenance/Equipment Operation......		
TOTAL FTEs Needed................		

PROJECT NOTES:

EMPHASIS: CHS CRP CM OI TOT

TYPE: CI DM TOT

DOI RANK: ....

OUTCOMES:

ES	WF	OMB	HEC	IAF	SDA	RW	FAR	PED	PRC	TOT
5	15	10	20	0	0	5		25	20	100

PLANNING LINK:

☒ Station CCP approved 10/97+   ☐ FWS Recovery Plan
☐ Station CCP/equivalent pre-10/97 ☒ FWS Ecosystem Goal/Plan
☒ Station Goal/Objective   ☐ Other Major Plan
☐ Station Step-down Mgmt Plan   ☐ Legal Mandate

This tour route will help meet goals and objectives listed in the various plans shown above.

RANK - STATION: ..0.0.5.. **DISTRICT:** .... **REGIONAL:** .... **NATIONAL:** ....

Updated October 9, 1998

```
21680    Little River NWR                                          OK
HQ: Little River NWR                              CD: OK03
Proj #: 98006          Type: NWR        District: Oklahoma
Main ecosystem: Arkansas/Red Rivers
```

ACTIVITY: *PUBLIC EDUCATION & RECREATION*   *People*
          7.a. Provide Visitor Services

MEASURES: 1,000 new visitors will be served
              2,000 existing visitors will be served
                  0 % will support the top 6 priority public uses
                  0 % will support non-priority public uses

TITLE:

DESCRIPTION:

Construct 24' X 10,000' (5.5 acres) of road in Unit 3 to provide public
access to the Refuge.

FUNDS NEEDED ($1000s):	One-Time	Recurring Base	First Year Need
Construction Costs...................	$300		
Operations: Personnel Cost..........			
Equipment Cost..........			
Facility Cost...........			
Services/Supplies.......			
Miscellaneous Costs.....			
TOTAL Operations Cost..			

PERMANENT STAFF NEEDED (FTEs):	Number (1/10s)	FTE Cost
Managers...............................		
Biologists............................		
Resource Specialists..................		
Education/Recreation Staff............		
Law Enforcement.......................		
Clerical/Administrative...............		
Maintenance/Equipment Operation.......		
TOTAL FTEs Needed..................		

PROJECT NOTES:

EMPHASIS: CHS CRP CM OI TOT **TYPE:** CI DM TOT **DOI RANK:** ....

OUTCOMES:

ES	WF	OMB	HEC	IAF	SDA	RW	FAR	PED	PRC	TOT
5	15	10	20	0	0	5		20	25	100

PLANNING LINK:

☒ Station CCP approved 10/97+   ☐ FWS Recovery Plan
☐ Station CCP/equivalent pre-10/97   ☐ FWS Ecosystem Goal/Plan
☒ Station Goal/Objective   ☐ Other Major Plan
☐ Station Step-down Mgmt Plan   ☐ Legal Mandate

This project will provide access for visitors to the Refuge in accordance with the objectives in the CMP.

RANK - STATION: ..0.0.6.. **DISTRICT:** .... **REGIONAL:** .... **NATIONAL:** ....

Updated October 9, 1998

HQ: Little River NWR   **CD:** OK03

Proj #: 98007   **Type:** NWR   **District:** Oklahoma

Main ecosystem: Arkansas/Red Rivers

ACTIVITY: *PUBLIC EDUCATION & RECREATION*   *People*

            7.a. Provide Visitor Services

MEASURES: 1,000 new visitors will be served

            2,000 existing visitors will be served

                  0 % will support the top 6 priority public uses

                  0 % will support non-priority public uses

TITLE:

DESCRIPTION:

Construct 24' X 18,500' (10 acres) of road in Unit 4 to provide public access to Refuge.

FUNDS NEEDED ($1000s):	One-Time	Recurring Base	First Year Need
Construction Costs...................	$30		
Operations: Personnel Cost..........			
Equipment Cost..........			
Facility Cost..........			
Services/Supplies.......			
Miscellaneous Costs.....			
TOTAL Operations Cost..			

PERMANENT STAFF NEEDED (FTEs):	Number (1/10s)	FTE Cost
Managers....................................		
Biologists.................................		
Resource Specialists.......................		
Education/Recreation Staff.................		
Law Enforcement............................		
Clerical/Administrative....................		
Maintenance/Equipment Operation............		
TOTAL FTEs Needed......................		

PROJECT NOTES:

EMPHASIS:	CHS	CRP	CM	OI	TOT	TYPE:	CI	DM	TOT	DOI RANK:

OUTCOMES:	ES	WF	OMB	HEC	IAF	SDA	RW	FAR	PED	PRC	TOT
	5	15	10	20	0	0	5		20	25	100

PLANNING LINK:

- ☒ Station CCP approved 10/97+
- ☐ Station CCP/equivalent pre-10/97
- ☒ Station Goal/Objective
- ☐ Station Step-down Mgmt Plan
- ☐ FWS Recovery Plan
- ☐ FWS Ecosystem Goal/Plan
- ☐ Other Major Plan
- ☐ Legal Mandate

This project will provide access for visitors to the Refuge in
accordance with the objectives shown in CMP.

RANK - STATION: ..007.. **DISTRICT:** .... **REGIONAL:** .... **NATIONAL:** ....

Updated October 9, 1998

21680 Little River NWR   OK

HQ: **Little River NWR**   CD: OK03

Proj #: 98008   **Type**: NWR   **District**: Oklahoma

Main ecosystem: Arkansas/Red Rivers

ACTIVITY: *PLANNING & ADMINISTRATION*   *Gen. Admin*
         8.b General Administration

MEASURES:

TITLE:

DESCRIPTION:

Headquarter facilities design and planning have been completed for the refuge. This project includes:

1. Headquarters and visitor contact station (5,000 sq. ft.)
2. Maintenance and storage building (4,000 sq. ft.)
3. Access road (24' X 2,000')
4. Parking area (20 cars and 2 buses)

FUNDS NEEDED ($1000s):

	One-Time	Recurring Base	First Year Need
Construction Costs...............	$5,000		
Operations: Personnel Cost.........			
Equipment Cost.........			
Facility Cost..........			
Services/Supplies.......			
Miscellaneous Costs.....			
TOTAL Operations Cost..			

PERMANENT STAFF NEEDED (FTEs):

	Number (1/10s)	FTE Cost
Managers.......................................		
Biologists.....................................		
Resource Specialists...........................		
Education/Recreation Staff.....................		
Law Enforcement................................		
Clerical/Administrative........................		
Maintenance/Equipment Operation...............		
TOTAL FTEs Needed......................		

PROJECT NOTES:

EMPHASIS: CHS CRP CM OI TOT

TYPE: CI DM TOT

DOI RANK: ....

OUTCOMES:

ES	WF	OMB	HEC	IAF	SDA	RW	FAR	PED	PRC	TOT
5	15	10	35	0	0	5		10	20	100

PLANNING LINK:

☒ Station CCP approved 10/97+   ☐ FWS Recovery Plan
☐ Station CCP/equivalent pre-10/97   ☒ FWS Ecosystem Goal/Plan
☒ Station Goal/Objective   ☐ Other Major Plan
☐ Station Step-down Mgmt Plan   ☐ Legal Mandate

This project will provide a central location on the Refuge for completing objectives described in documents noted above.

RANK - STATION: ..008.. **DISTRICT:** .... **REGIONAL:** .... **NATIONAL:** ....

Updated October 9, 1998

21680 Little River NWR   OK

HQ: Little River NWR   **CD:** OK03

Proj #: 98009   **Type:** NWR   **District:** Oklahoma

Main ecosystem: Arkansas/Red Rivers

ACTIVITY: *PUBLIC EDUCATION & RECREATION*   *People*

7.a. Provide Visitor Services

MEASURES: 2,000 new visitors will be served

1,000 existing visitors will be served

0 % will support the top 6 priority public uses

0 % will support non-priority public uses

TITLE:

DESCRIPTION:

Construct public restroom in Unit 2 near headquarters and visitor contact station.

FUNDS NEEDED ($1000s):	One-Time	Recurring Base	First Year Need
Construction Costs...................	$50		
Operations: Personnel Cost..........			
Equipment Cost..........			
Facility Cost..........			
Services/Supplies.......			
Miscellaneous Costs.....			
TOTAL Operations Cost..			

PERMANENT STAFF NEEDED (FTEs):	Number (1/10s)	FTE Cost
Managers..		
Biologists......................................		
Resource Specialists............................		
Education/Recreation Staff......................		
Law Enforcement.................................		
Clerical/Administrative.........................		
Maintenance/Equipment Operation.................		
TOTAL FTEs Needed...........................		

PROJECT NOTES:

EMPHASIS:	CHS	CRP	CM	OI	TOT		TYPE:	CI	DM	TOT		DOI RANK:

OUTCOMES:	ES	WF	OMB	HEC	IAF	SDA	RW	FAR	PED	PRC	TOT
	0	0	0	0	0	0	0		0	100	100

PLANNING LINK:

☒ Station CCP approved 10/97+   ☐ FWS Recovery Plan
☐ Station CCP/equivalent pre-10/97 ☐ FWS Ecosystem Goal/Plan
☐ Station Goal/Objective   ☐ Other Major Plan
☐ Station Step-down Mgmt Plan   ☐ Legal Mandate

Visitors to the Refuge will need sanitary facilities.

RANK - STATION: 009   **DISTRICT:** ....   **REGIONAL:** ....   **NATIONAL:** ....

Updated October 9, 1998

```
21680    Little River NWR                                              OK
HQ: Little River NWR                                    CD: OK03
Proj #: 98010        Type: NWR          District: Oklahoma
Main ecosystem: Arkansas/Red Rivers
```

┌───┐
│   │
└───┘

ACTIVITY: *PUBLIC EDUCATION & RECREATION*   *People*
          7.a. Provide Visitor Services

MEASURES: 1,000 new visitors will be served
               2,000 existing visitors will be served
                    0 % will support the top 6 priority public uses
                    0 % will support non-priority public uses

TITLE:

DESCRIPTION:
Develop a hiking trail in Unit 2.

FUNDS NEEDED ($1000s):	One-Time	Recurring Base	First Year Need
Construction Costs....................	$20		
Operations: Personnel Cost..........			
Equipment Cost..........			
Facility Cost..........			
Services/Supplies.......			
Miscellaneous Costs.....			
TOTAL Operations Cost..			

PERMANENT STAFF NEEDED (FTEs):	Number (1/10s)	FTE Cost
Managers.................................		
Biologists...............................		
Resource Specialists.....................		
Education/Recreation Staff...............		
Law Enforcement..........................		
Clerical/Administrative..................		
Maintenance/Equipment Operation..........		
TOTAL FTEs Needed........................		

PROJECT NOTES:

EMPHASIS:

CHS	CRP	CM	OI	TOT

TYPE:

CI	DM	TOT

DOI RANK: ....

OUTCOMES:

ES	WF	OMB	HEC	IAF	SDA	RW	FAR	PED	PRC	TOT
0	0	0	0	0	0	0		50	50	100

PLANNING LINK:

☒ Station CCP approved 10/97+ ☐ FWS Recovery Plan
☐ Station CCP/equivalent pre-10/97 ☒ FWS Ecosystem Goal/Plan
☐ Station Goal/Objective ☐ Other Major Plan
☐ Station Step-down Mgmt Plan ☐ Legal Mandate

Construction of an interpretative hiking trail in Unit 2 will provide
visitors with an appreciation of wildlife and its habitat.

RANK - STATION: ..010.. **DISTRICT:** .... **REGIONAL:** .... **NATIONAL:** ....

Updated October 9, 1998

HQ: **Little River NWR**   CD: OK03

Proj #: 98011   **Type:** NWR   **District:** Oklahoma

Main ecosystem: Arkansas/Red Rivers

ACTIVITY: *PUBLIC EDUCATION & RECREATION*   *People*

　　　　7.a. Provide Visitor Services

MEASURES:　　　1,000 new visitors will be served

　　　　　　　500 existing visitors will be served

　　　　　　　　0 % will support the top 6 priority public uses

　　　　　　　　0 % will support non-priority public uses

TITLE:

DESCRIPTION:

Construct boat ramp and access road south of headquarters and visitor
contact station. One mile of road with gravel top in Unit 2.

FUNDS NEEDED ($1000s):

	One-Time	Recurring Base	First Year Need
Construction Costs...................	$75		
Operations: Personnel Cost..........			
Equipment Cost..........			
Facility Cost...........			
Services/Supplies.......			
Miscellaneous Costs.....			
TOTAL Operations Cost..			

PERMANENT STAFF NEEDED (FTEs):

	Number (1/10s)	FTE Cost
Managers...................................		
Biologists.................................		
Resource Specialists.......................		
Education/Recreation Staff.................		
Law Enforcement............................		
Clerical/Administrative....................		
Maintenance/Equipment Operation............		
TOTAL FTEs Needed..................		

PROJECT NOTES:

EMPHASIS:	CHS	CRP	CM	OI	TOT		TYPE:	CI	DM	TOT		DOI RANK:

	ES	WF	OMB	HEC	IAF	SDA	RW	FAR	PED	PRC	TOT
OUTCOMES:	0	0	0	0	0	0	0		0	100	100

PLANNING LINK:

- ☒ Station CCP approved 10/97+
- ☐ Station CCP/equivalent pre-10/97
- ☐ Station Goal/Objective
- ☐ Station Step-down Mgmt Plan
- ☐ FWS Recovery Plan
- ☐ FWS Ecosystem Goal/Plan
- ☐ Other Major Plan
- ☐ Legal Mandate

This facility will provide safe easy access to Little River in accordance with objectives outlined in the station CMP.

RANK - STATION: 011   **DISTRICT:**   **REGIONAL:**   **NATIONAL:**

Updated October 9, 1998

HQ: Little River NWR   **CD: OK03**

Proj #: 98012   **Type:** NWR   **District:** Oklahoma

Main ecosystem: Arkansas/Red Rivers

ACTIVITY: *PUBLIC EDUCATION & RECREATION*   *People*

        7.a. Provide Visitor Services

MEASURES: 4,000 new visitors will be served

        2,000 existing visitors will be served

               0 % will support the top 6 priority public uses

               0 % will support non-priority public uses

TITLE:

DESCRIPTION:

Develop pullouts for wildlife observation on auto tour route in Unit 2.

FUNDS NEEDED ($1000s):

	One-Time	Recurring Base	First Year Need
Construction Costs..................	$10		
Operations: Personnel Cost.........			
Equipment Cost.........			
Facility Cost...........			
Services/Supplies.......			
Miscellaneous Costs.....			
TOTAL Operations Cost..			

PERMANENT STAFF NEEDED (FTEs):

	Number (1/10s)	FTE Cost
Managers...............................		
Biologists.............................		
Resource Specialists...................		
Education/Recreation Staff.............		
Law Enforcement........................		
Clerical/Administrative................		
Maintenance/Equipment Operation........		
TOTAL FTEs Needed..................		

PROJECT NOTES:

EMPHASIS:

CHS	CRP	CM	OI	TOT

TYPE:

CI	DM	TOT

DOI RANK: ....

OUTCOMES:

ES	WF	OMB	HEC	IAF	SDA	RW	FAR	PED	PRC	TOT
5	15	10	20	0	0	5		20	25	100

PLANNING LINK:

☒ Station CCP approved 10/97+   ☐ FWS Recovery Plan
☐ Station CCP/equivalent pre-10/97   ☒ FWS Ecosystem Goal/Plan
☐ Station Goal/Objective   ☐ Other Major Plan
☐ Station Step-down Mgmt Plan   ☐ Legal Mandate

This project will provide educational and recreational opportunities
to the Refuge visitors in accordance with goals and objectives
outlined in above documents.

RANK - STATION: ..012.. **DISTRICT:** .... **REGIONAL:** .... **NATIONAL:** ....

Updated October 9, 1998

```
21680   Little River NWR                                          OK
HQ: Little River NWR                              CD: OK03
Proj #: 98013        Type: NWR      District: Oklahoma
Main ecosystem: Arkansas/Red Rivers
```

┌───┐
│   │
└───┘

ACTIVITY: *HABITAT RESTORATION*   *Habitat*
            2.a. Wetland Restoration

MEASURES: 100 refuge acres will be restored
                    0 off-refuge acres will be restored

TITLE:

DESCRIPTION:

An experimental moist soil unit will be constructed in Unit 2 covering
100 acres using low level dikes and rain fall as a water source.

FUNDS NEEDED ($1000s):

	One-Time	Recurring Base	First Year Need
Construction Costs..................	$50		
Operations: Personnel Cost..........			
Equipment Cost.........			
Facility Cost..........			
Services/Supplies.......			
Miscellaneous Costs.....			
TOTAL Operations Cost..			

PERMANENT STAFF NEEDED (FTEs):

	Number (1/10s)	FTE Cost
Managers....................................		
Biologists.................................		
Resource Specialists.......................		
Education/Recreation Staff.................		
Law Enforcement............................		
Clerical/Administrative....................		
Maintenance/Equipment Operation............		
TOTAL FTEs Needed......................		

PROJECT NOTES:

EMPHASIS: CHS CRP CM OI TOT

TYPE: CI DM TOT

DOI RANK: ....

ES	WF	OMB	HEC	IAF	SDA	RW	FAR	PED	PRC	TOT
OUTCOMES: 5	45	20	10	0	0	0		15	5	100

PLANNING LINK:

☒ Station CCP approved 10/97+   ☐ FWS Recovery Plan
☐ Station CCP/equivalent pre-10/97 ☒ FWS Ecosystem Goal/Plan
☒ Station Goal/Objective   ☐ Other Major Plan
☐ Station Step-down Mgmt Plan   ☐ Legal Mandate

This experimental project in Unit 2 will be monitored for success in enhancing the area for waterfowl. If successful more similar projects will be developed in other units.

RANK - STATION: ..013..   **DISTRICT:** ....   **REGIONAL:** ....   **NATIONAL:** ....

Updated October 9, 1998

Little River
National Wildlife Refuge

Environmental
Assessment

November 1998

U.S. FISH AND WILDLIFE SERVICE
ENVIRONMENTAL ACTION MEMORANDUM

Within the spirit and intent of the Council on Environmental Quality's regulations for implementing the National Environmental Policy Act (NEPA) and other statutes, orders, and policies that protect fish and wildlife resources, I have established the following administrative record and have determined that the action of approval of proposals reflected in the The Little River National Wildlife Refuge Comprehensive Conservation Plan and in the preferred alternative identified in the associated Environmental Assessment:

_____   is a categorical exclusion as provided by 516 DM 6 Appendix 1 section B(4). No further documentation will be made.

__X__   is found not to have significant environmental effects as determined by the attached Environmental Assessment and Finding of No Significant Impact.

_____   is found to have special environmental conditions as described in the attached Environmental Assessment. The attached Finding of No Significant Impact will not be final nor any actions taken pending a 30 day period for public review (40 CFR 1501.4(e)(2)).

_____   is found to have significant effects, and therefore a "Notice of Intent" will be published in the Federal Register to prepare an Environmental Impact Statement before the project is considered further.

_____   is denied because of environmental damage, Service policy, or mandate.

_____   is an emergency situation. Only those actions necessary to control the immediate impacts of the emergency will be taken. Other related actions remain subject to NEPA review.

Attachments: Other supporting documents: Finding of No Significant Impact, Little River NWR Comprehensive Conservation Plan and Environmental Assessment.

Nancy M. Kaufman 12/30/98
Regional Director   Date

(1) _April E. Fletcher_ 12-11-98
Initiator   Date

(2) _Lynn B. Stauer_ 12/15/98
Geographic ARD, OK/TX   Date

(3) _David M. Dell_ 12/13/98
Nepa Coordinator, Region 2   Date

U.S. Fish and Wildlife Service
Little River National Wildlife Refuge
Broken Bow, Oklahoma

FINDING OF NO SIGNIFICANT IMPACT

APPROVAL OF LITTLE RIVER NATIONAL WILDLIFE REFUGE COMPREHENSIVE CONSERVATION PLAN

The U.S. Fish and Wildlife Service proposes to approve for implementation, a long-term Comprehensive Conservation Plan to guide the management of Little River National Wildlife Refuge over the next 10 to 15 years. The Plan identifies goals and objectives for the Refuge, and strategies to achieve those goals and objectives, as described in the attached Environmental Assessment and Draft Comprehensive Conservation Plan.

The Service has analyzed alternatives to the present and future management of the Refuge, and through this process has identified the following conservation plan alternatives:

1. No action. Continue Refuge management and public use programs as currently operating.

2. Non-management. Close the Refuge to all public use. Do no active habitat improvement. Allow nature to take its course and bottomland hardwood forests to recover through natural succession of altered areas.

3. Minimal habitat manipulation, moderate increase in public use, and some improvement of public use facilities (Preferred Alternative) This alternative would provide for an increase in waterfowl and shorebird habitat and improvement of public use facilities to accommodate a moderate increase in use. It also calls for continuation of existing hunting programs, identified in the Comprehensive Conservation Plan.

4. Full development and intensive management. This alternative would accommodate major increases in public and recreational uses, and full intensive management to maximize speed of recovery of bottomland hardwood forest.

The Preferred Alternative was selected over the other alternatives because it meets the needs both of the Refuge and of the public, while providing for long-term restoration and protection of the bottomland hardwood forest of the Refuge and its associated wildlife. Alternatives 1 and 2 do not meet those needs, and Alternative 4 anticipates public needs which current trends do not

1

indicate will materialize, and provides for habitat expansion that may not be required for the restoration and maintenance of the Refuge's bottomland forests and wildlife.

The Preferred Alternative allows for conservative improvements in habitat management and public use facilities after evaluation of specific need, potential impact, and evaluation of alternatives and results of actions. It provides flexibility to adapt to changing financial resources, while permitting steady, long-term maintenance and/or improvement of wildlife habitat and public use programs and facilities.

The Preferred Alternative was selected based on extensive evaluation of the biotic and abiotic resources of the Refuge and the impact of potential management actions and current and potential public use needs. This alternative recognizes the need for, and provides for monitoring and flexibility to meet changing conditions and permit adjustment of actions based upon acquisition of new data. The Preferred Alternative provides that flexibility, while providing focus for the long-term management of the Refuge. It provides for the evaluation under the NEPA process of any major actions believed to be needed based on data acquired.

Therefore, it is my determination that implementing the Preferred Alternative 3 does not constitute a major Federal action significantly affecting the human environment. As such, an Environmental Impact Statement is not required.

Nancy M. Kaufman 12/30/98
Regional Director, Region 2   Date
U.S. Fish and Wildlife Service

Little River National Wildlife Refuge
Environmental Assessment

I. Purpose

The purpose of this Comprehensive Conservation Plan for Little River National Wildlife Refuge is to facilitate the restoration, maintenance, and management of bottomland hardwood forest habitat to enhance wildlife for the benefit of people, and to facilitate continuity of management and sound decision-making to achieve these ends. The plan is intended to provide for long-term management based on careful consideration of the physical and biological characteristics of the Refuge, and to ensure long-term needs of the Refuge and the habitat are met. It is designed to facilitate achievement of U.S. Fish and Wildlife Service and Refuge goals, provide for protection of wildlife and its habitat, provide for appropriate and compatible public recreation, and promote public appreciation of the bottomland hardwood ecosystem and its components.

II. Needs

This action is designed to address both the needs of the Service to meet its responsibilities and the needs of the local community and the general public.

The Service has responsibility for stewardship over endangered species and migratory birds, as well as other species that occupy Service lands. The Refuge was established February 10, 1987 as "an inviolate sanctuary . . . for migratory birds" (16 U.S.C. 715d) and for "the conservation of . . . wetlands . . . and to help fulfill international obligations contained in various migratory bird treaties and conventions" (16 U.S.C. 3901(b)). In addition, the Refuge was established ". . . for the development, advancement, management, conservation, and protection of fish and wildlife resources . . ." (16 U.S.C. 742(b)(1)).

To meet its responsibilities, the Service needs to provide for the protection and restoration of bottomland hardwoods for wildlife habitat, and provide for protection of the wildlife that uses that habitat. The Service also needs to ensure that all recreational activities occurring on the Refuge are compatible with the purposes for which the Refuge was established. To facilitate management and ensure these ends are achieved, the Service needs to develop plans which will maximize the cost/benefit ratio of management actions.

The needs of the public, primarily the local area communities, are for a place where traditional recreational activities, such as fishing, hunting, and observing wildlife can be enjoyed. Since most of the privately owned

1

hardwood forests of the Little River floodplain have been altered for commercial purposes, hunting opportunities have been lost. Refuge lands are among the few places remaining where river access is available and hunting opportunities still remain. The Oklahoma House of Representatives and Senate authorized establishment of the Refuge provided ". . . that the United States Fish and Wildlife Service shall enter into a cooperative agreement with the Oklahoma Department of Wildlife Conservation to allow hunting in such waterfowl refuge."[1]

III. Alternatives Including Proposed Action

Alternative 1: No Action

The No Action Alternative would continue current management practices. These are outlined in detail in the Comprehensive Conservation Plan under "Current Status" in the Objective Documentation section. In summary, this alternative would result in access roads remaining as they are and recreational programs would continue to be limited to those provided for under existing, approved hunting plans. No public informational signs would be posted and viewing opportunities for the non-hunting/fishing public would remain limited. No active habitat management to accelerate the rate of restoration of bottomland hardwoods would occur. Management actions that protect wildlife habitat, such as beaver control and law enforcement activities, would continue. This alternative would assume no significant increase in public use.

Alternative 2: Non-management

This alternative would close the Refuge entirely to the public through closure of all access roads. The Refuge has no control over boats on the river, but access to Refuge lands from the river would be denied by closing all boat launch sites. There would be no effort to control beaver or other naturally occurring species. No active habitat improvement would be done. Management would consist only of road maintenance on those roads needed by Refuge staff to ensure enforcement of the Refuge closure. Nature would be allowed to take its course and bottomland hardwood forests to recover through natural invasion of altered areas.

---

[1] House Joint Resolution #1046, signed by Governor George Nigh, March 31, 1986

This option was not considered viable due to the agreement with the State of Oklahoma that recreational opportunities would be provided on the Refuge.

Alternative 3: Minimal habitat manipulation, moderate increase in public use, and some improvement of public use facilities (Preferred Alternative)

Under this alternative, existing roads would be maintained and improved, and roads would be expanded as necessary to accommodate increasing recreational use of the Refuge. Any impacts on water flow patterns resulting from road construction/improvement would be mitigated. As recreational use of the Refuge increased, improvements would be made to accommodate the additional traffic, including expanded parking areas and automobile pull-outs, and informational/ educational signs would be provided. The Refuge would conduct outreach to expand public knowledge of the values of bottomland hardwood forests.

Habitat loss for road improvement would involve only a few acres. There would be minor loss of habitat for road widening. In some pine forest areas where recovery of bottomland species occurs slowly, actions would be taken to accelerate that recovery. To enhance habitat for shorebirds and other species that prefer open water, 20 acres would be converted to experimental green tree reservoirs and a 100-acre impoundment would be constructed. Beaver and other animals would be controlled as necessary to prevent irreversible habitat damage.

Hunting programs would remaining at existing, approved levels. Rabbit and squirrel hunting would continue throughout the Refuge, but would be phased out of Unit 2 as other non-hunting recreational use increased. Limited hunting programs for deer, waterfowl, turkey and raccoon would be offered each year.

Implementation of major management actions would require additional environmental evaluation and National Environmental Policy Act documentation.

Alternative 4: Full development and intensive management

This alternative would involve construction of a visitor center, an extensive trail system with signage, and development of other programs. It would also involve extensive habitat manipulation, including construction of numerous acres of green tree reservoirs and other impoundments to significantly expand habitat for mallards, wood ducks, and other waterfowl.

A visitor center would expand public use of the Refuge. There would be increasing potential for interest in the Refuge from people using

Highways 70 and 259 on their way to other recreation sites in the area, such as Beavers Bend State Park and Broken Bow Lake.

This alternative was originally considered by management in 1990. However, although it is evaluated here for its environmental impacts, it is no longer considered a viable alternative at this time in light of existing and anticipated budgetary constraints. When originally considered, it was anticipated there would be a growing local population and rapidly increasing traffic on Highways 70 and 259. In reality, the local population has remained relatively unchanged since 1990, and highway traffic increase has not been as great as previously expected.

IV. Affected Environment

The Refuge is located almost entirely within the floodplain of Little River, which generally delineates its southern boundary. Most of the exterior boundary of the Refuge has been established, but several private inholdings still remain that are planned for acquisition as the lands and funds become available (see map, Appendix A). The Refuge lands are a mosaic of regenerated bottomland forest, pine plantations, dense brush, and young upland hardwood forests, intermixed with streams, oxbows, and beaver ponds.

The bottomland forest ecosystem is dynamic, with periodic flooding keeping lower elevations continually in flux due to changing patterns of erosion and deposition of soils. Plant communities vary depending on elevation, soil saturation, and the stages of succession. Historically, the plant associations ranged from permanently flooded cypress communities to periodically flooded oak-hickory woodlands. Existing plant species generally are adapted to the periodic flooding of the river.

The Refuge offers a diversity of wildlife. It is home to a number of game species including mallards, wood ducks, other waterfowl, white-tailed deer, raccoons, wild turkey, swamp rabbits, and grey squirrels. The Refuge is an important migration stop for many species of neotropical birds. It provides suitable nesting habitat for herons, egrets, anhingas, and Swainson's warblers as well as other species of special significance such as the American alligator, the bird-voiced treefrog, and mole salamander.

Bald eagles, federally listed as threatened, overwinter in southeastern Oklahoma. They generally arrive in McCurtain County in December and leave during March. Up to six bald eagles have been observed on the Refuge during a season.

A full description of the Refuge, its resources, and its socioeconomic setting are included in the Comprehensive Conservation Plan.

V. Environmental
Consequences

Implementation of any of the options identified, except #2 (non-management), would assume that public access into the Refuge could be obtained as needed.

Alternative 1: No Action

Implementing the No Action alternative would assume no significant increase in recreational use of the Refuge. Due to existing limited legal access over privately owned roads, any significant increase in traffic would probably require acquisition of additional right-of-ways into Refuge lands. There has been an increase in use of recreational sites in the area. It is reasonable to assume that the lack of signs indicating the presence of the Refuge and the lack of public facilities on the Refuge explain why there has been no increase in numbers of visitors on the Refuge.

Impacts on Wildlife and Habitat Management: Under this alternative, ducks, deer, raccoons, squirrels and rabbits would be hunted on the Refuge. These species reproduce rapidly, and their populations are not believed to be suffering adverse impacts as a result of hunting.

Fishing would continue to occur in the waters of the Refuge using existing primitive boat launches and parking areas. Species fished would include largemouth bass, spotted bass, channel catfish, and flathead catfish. Since the river waters of the Refuge where this fishing occurs are not excluded from the remaining Little River waters, natural recruitment would replenish populations. Impacts would result primarily from anglers traveling to and from fishing areas. These impacts would be minimized by controlling access and limiting travel to selected roads and trails. Impacts on habitat would generally occur in the immediate vicinity of small, existing parking areas.

Since the existing Upland Game and Fishing Plan has been in place, there have been no known negative impacts on wildlife or fish populations or on habitat except for minor impacts resulting from small clearing areas where cars are parked for fishing.

Under this alternative, there would be no construction of additional impoundments, so waterfowl populations would not be expected to increase significantly. Bottomland hardwood species would naturally invade pine plantation areas, but no effort would be made to accelerate that invasion and restoration of the bottomland hardwood forest.

Impacts on Endangered and Threatened Species: Little or no impacts on listed species are anticipated under current management practices. Existing hunting and fishing programs have no impacts on bald eagle use of Refuge habitat, as noted in a compatibility determination. The reasons are (1) that hunters normally use areas different from those used by eagles (woodland versus open water), (2) eagles are sparse and distributed over a large area, and (3) fishing has negligible impacts on forage fish used by eagles.

Although the American alligator occurs on the Refuge, the population is small. Conflicts with hunting are minimized since alligators generally hibernate during most of the months when Refuge hunting seasons are open. No significant impacts on alligator populations as a result of fishing are anticipated.

A small population of the endangered Ouachita rock pocketbook mussel inhabits riffles in Little River. Boating and fishing should cause no problem to them because, due to the shallowness of the water, boats generally shut off motors while going over the riffle areas to avoid damage to propellers. Changes in hydrology and water temperatures in the Little River have probably had a more significant impact on the remaining rock pocketbook mussels than boating.

Impacts on Air and Water Quality: This alternative would have no impact on air quality. Automobile traffic through the Refuge would not be at levels that could result in measurable air pollution. Water quality may be affected to a minor degree by pollution from the use of motor boats. Waterflow would not be affected by construction of impoundments.

Impacts on Aesthetic and Visual Resources: Nothing would change from the current conditions except natural changes resulting from continuing growth of bottomland hardwoods.

Impacts on Archeological and Historical Resources: This alternative would have no known impact on archeological and historical resources.

Impacts on Socioeconomic Resources: This alternative provides for continuation of existing hunting and fishing opportunities for local citizens. An increase in use of the area by local citizens is not anticipated in the near future since the county population has declined by 7.5 percent (3,000 people) in the past 10 years. An increase in tourism in the vicinity would not be likely to result from an increase in Refuge public use since there are no facilities on the Refuge to accommodate, nor signs to attract, additional visitors.

Alternative 2: Non-management Alternative

Under this alternative, bottomland hardwoods would be allowed to regenerate naturally. There would be no hunting, fishing, or other public use allowed, and no active management of wildlife except enforcement of the Refuge closure. This was not considered a viable option since the State of Oklahoma authorized acquisition of the Refuge with the understanding that the Service would provide hunting opportunities.[2]

Alternative 3: Minimal Habitat Manipulation, Moderate Increase in Public Use, and Some Improvement of Public Use Facilities (Preferred Alternative)

Fully implementing this alternative would require acquisition of additional right-of-ways and improved road access. Full implementation would depend upon availability of funds.

Impacts on Wildlife and Habitat Management: This alternative offers the best opportunities to actively manage for wildlife and habitat with minimal impacts on wetlands and wildlife habitat. Accelerating restoration of bottomland hardwood species through removal of pine plantations would provide quality habitat for wildlife more quickly than under Alternative 1. Construction of additional impoundments would allow an increase in habitat for waterfowl and other aquatic species.

Construction of additional roads or improvement of road access could have minor negative impacts on wildlife through loss of several acres of habitat and minor disturbance of wildlife during road construction and from increased public use. If access were acquired along existing road prints, habitat loss would consist of an additional 10 to 15 feet adjacent to the road print. If access were constructed where no road print exists, there could be habitat loss along a strip approximately 35 feet wide. Potential disturbance of wildlife in public viewing areas could be mitigated by constructing viewing blinds, and habitat loss could be mitigated with improvements in other areas. The actual environmental impacts of alternatives for access improvement/development would have to be evaluated and reviewed under provisions of the National Environmental Policy Act prior to construction.

Hunting programs would have minor impacts on wildlife. The hunts are designed to cause minimal disturbance to non-hunted species. Monitoring of hunted species would ensure early detection of any unanticipated negative impacts on populations.

Impacts on Endangered and Threatened Species: Under this alternative, listed species would be provided added protection through increased surveillance and law enforcement. Also under this alternative, federally designated threatened and endangered species that may use the Refuge

---

[2] See footnote 1, page 2.

7

would be identified and management actions would be taken to protect them and to enhance their habitats.

Impacts on Air and Water Quality: Air pollution might show localized minor increases due to increased automobile traffic and related exhaust emissions. Negligible increases in water pollution could result from use of motor boats on the river. However, those impacts would be evaluated prior to construction and/or improvement of roads, road access, parking areas, and expansion of right-of-ways. At that time, evaluation would determine impacts, and mitigation measures needed in accordance with the National Environmental Policy Act.

Impacts on Aesthetic and Visual Resources: The aesthetic and visual impacts of this alternative would be both positive and negative. Improvement of existing access roads, and development of new roads and pull-outs at strategic locations would enhance public viewing opportunities. Some areas would be more visible due to clearing, resulting in improved visibility. Erecting informational signs, widening roads, and constructing small parking areas and pull-outs could have negative visual impacts. In either case, the impacts would be minimal, considering the total area of the Refuge that would be affected.

Impacts on Cultural and Historical Resources: Potential impacts on cultural and historical resources are unknown. They must be determined prior to widening of access roads and construction of a visitor contact station and parking lots within the Refuge. At the time such widening and/or construction would occur, the potential impact of all alternatives would be evaluated and mitigation measures would be taken.

Impacts on Socioeconomic Resources: Improvement of recreational opportunities on the Refuge would have positive impacts on local businesses through increased recreational activity. With improvements such as proper signing, additional people would be attracted into the Refuge who might then use local businesses for purchase of recreational equipment and supplies.

Hunting programs will have seasonal impacts on recreational users. The improvement of parking, pull-outs, and informational signage would provide opportunities for local school use as well as non-consumptive recreational users of the Refuge.

Alternative 4: Full Development and Intensive Management

Implementation of this alternative would require acquisition of right-of-ways for increased vehicle access plus water, power, and telephone lines.

Impacts on Wildlife and Habitat Management: This alternative would maximize waterfowl habitat with possible detrimental affects on other species that would lose habitat. Numerous impoundments would be constructed to enhance waterfowl populations on the refuge, which could impact other waterfowl use patterns in the area. Attracting waterfowl away from other areas would not provide substantial benefit to waterfowl populations, and could affect waterfowl hunting in other locations.

Managing primarily for waterfowl and specific wildlife production would be counterproductive to the current Service policy of managing ecosystems for a diversity of wildlife.

Impacts on Endangered, Threatened, and Candidate Species: Impacts on listed species generally would be similar to those occurring under Preferred Alternative 3. However, implementation of this alternative could result in significant human disturbance of bald eagles and other threatened and endangered species that may use the bottomland hardwoods and waters of the Refuge. Increased open water, however, could benefit bald eagles.

Impacts on Air and Water Quality: A high volume of vehicle and boat traffic through the Refuge could have minor detrimental impact on vegetation and water during heavy use periods due to accompanying air pollution and oil leakage. These impacts, however, would be periodic, with recovery possible between periods of high use.

Impacts on Aesthetic and Visual Resources: Development of the Refuge would reduce the natural atmosphere that many visitors seek. Open vistas may be degraded by installation of a parking area or directional signs.

Impacts on Cultural and Historic Resources: Impacts on cultural and historic resources would be evaluated at the time of construction of roads, visitor center, parking areas, and boat launches. However, development most likely would have little or no impact.

Impacts on Socioeconomic Resources: High public use of the Refuge could have a positive impact on local businesses by increasing the probability that visitors would stop in local communities to shop, buy supplies, gasoline, etc.

VI. Consultation and Coordination

The planning process for Little River National Wildlife Refuge began shortly after establishment of the Refuge with a public scoping meeting in Broken Bow, Oklahoma, on October 12, 1988. A draft was nearing completion in 1991, but due to loss of staff, it was set aside and was not picked up again until planning staff were added in 1995. By that time, a great deal had changed and much more had been learned about the Refuge which made it imperative to re-write the draft with major revisions. Since scoping had already been conducted, it seemed more appropriate to complete the revised draft and make it available for public review and comment rather than to go out for another scoping meeting. The draft was subsequently revised and made available to the public, and a second meeting was held on March 6, 1997 in Broken Bow, Oklahoma to get public comment. Comments received were overwhelmingly for changes permitting additional hunting opportunities on the refuge. As a result, again major revisions were made in the draft. Because those changes were also significant, a second draft was subsequently made available for public review and comment. In the interim, the Refuge also prepared plans to open up the Refuge to additional hunting opportunities, and made those plans available for public comment prior to finalizing as well.

Service staff, agencies and companies that contributed to the preparation of this plan include: *April Fletcher*, Refuge Planner, U.S. Fish and Wildlife Service; *Berlin Heck*, Manager, Little River National Wildlife Refuge; *Joseph P. Mazzoni*, Former Assistant Regional Director, Refuges and Wildlife; *Bill Howe*, Nongame Migratory Bird Coordinator, U.S. Fish and Wildlife Service; *Jerry Brabander*, Tulsa Ecological Services Field Office, U.S. Fish and Wildlife Service; *Doug St. Pierre*, Former Realty Specialist, U.S. Fish and Wildife Service; *Oklahoma Department of Wildlife Conservation; Forestry Services, Oklahoma Department of Agriculture; and Weyerhaueser Corporation.*

VII. Bibliography

Brabander, J.J., Masters, R.E., and Short, R.M. 1985. U.S. Fish and Wildlife Service. Bottomland Hardwoods of Eastern Oklahoma: A Special Study of Their Status, Trends and Values.

McMahan, C.A, and Frye, R.G., Eds. 1986. Bottomland Hardwoods in Texas: Proceedings of an Interagency Workshop on Status and Ecology, May 6-7, 1986, Nacogdoches, Texas. 170pp.

Roelle, J.E., Auble, G.T., Hamilton D.B., Johnson, R.L., and Segelquist, C.A. 1987. U.S. Fish and Wildlife Service, National Ecology Center. Results of a Workshop Concerning Ecological Zonation in Bottomland Hardwoods.

U.S. Department of Agriculture. Forest Service. 1978. Bottomland Hardwood Preservation Program, Lower Mississippi River Delta, Habitat Category 7. Atlanta, Georgia.

U.S. Department of Agriculture. Soil Conservation Service, in cooperation with Oklahoma Agricultural Experiment Station. Soil Survey, McCurtain County, Oklahoma. 1974. U.S. Govt. Printing Office, Washington, D.C. 10430.

U.S. Department of the Interior. U.S. Fish and Wildlife Service. 1985. Land Protection Plan: Texas/Oklahoma Bottomland Hardwoods, Migratory Waterfowl, Category 3. Albuquerque, New Mexico.

U.S. Department of the Interior. U.S. Fish and Wildlife Service.1986. Proposed Protection of Little River Area Bottomland Hardwoods. Final Environmental Assessment. Washington, D.C.

U.S. Department of the Interior. U.S. Fish and Wildlife Service. 1988.Upland Game and Fishing Plan, Little River National Wildlife Refuge, McCurtain County, Oklahoma. Broken Bow, Oklahoma.

www.ingramcontent.com/pod-product-compliance
Lightning Source LLC
Chambersburg PA
CBHW081215280526

45787CB00006B/2415